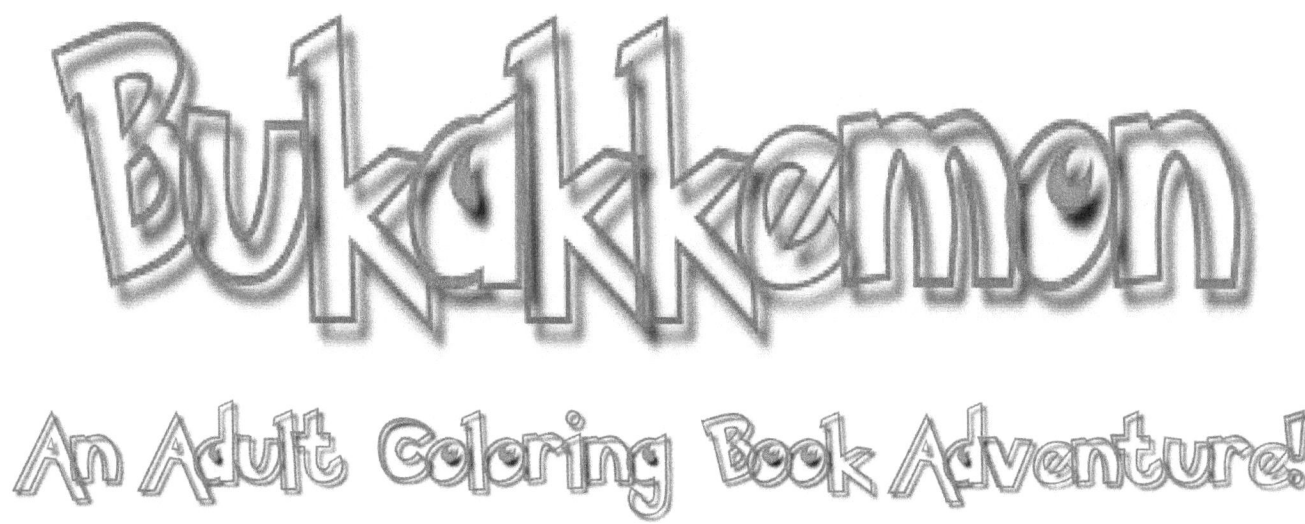

Bukakkemon

An Adult Coloring Book Adventure!

Alexis Hex

Welcome to the Sloppiho Region.

Adventurer we need your assistance.
There as been an outbreak of infectious creatures
known as Bukakkemon.

Please head directly to the free clinic and find
Prof. Thirst.

He will give you all the information you need.

Greetings I'm Prof. Thirst. Thank you for coming.

The Bukakkemon outbreak has gotten out of control.

I need your help to put together my report for the center of disease control.

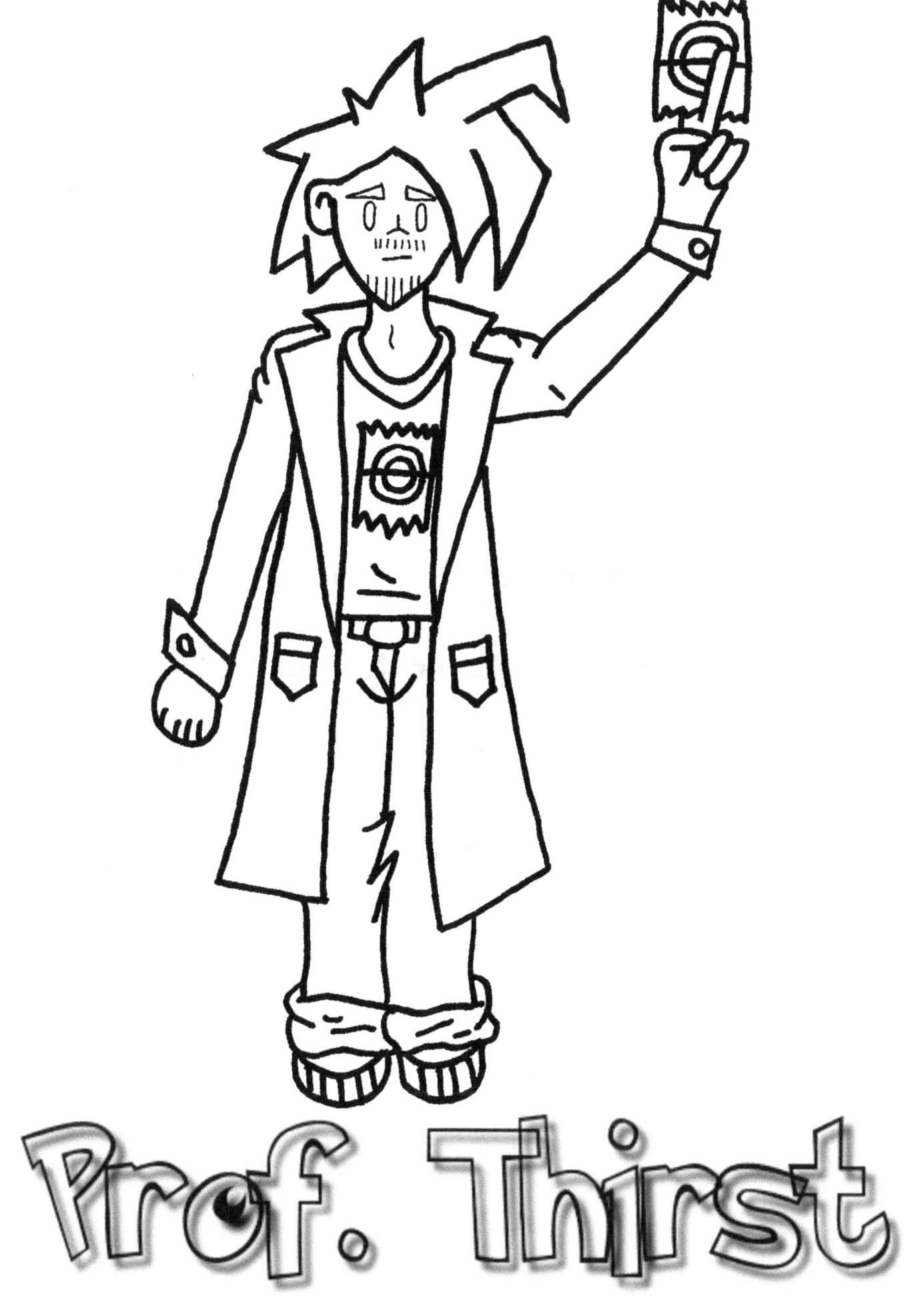

Prof. Thirst

Take some of these Condominators.

Simply rip open the wrapper to catch a Bukakkemon.

If you need more stop in at any free clinic.

Good luck!

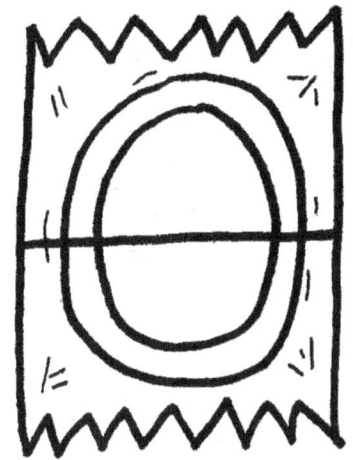
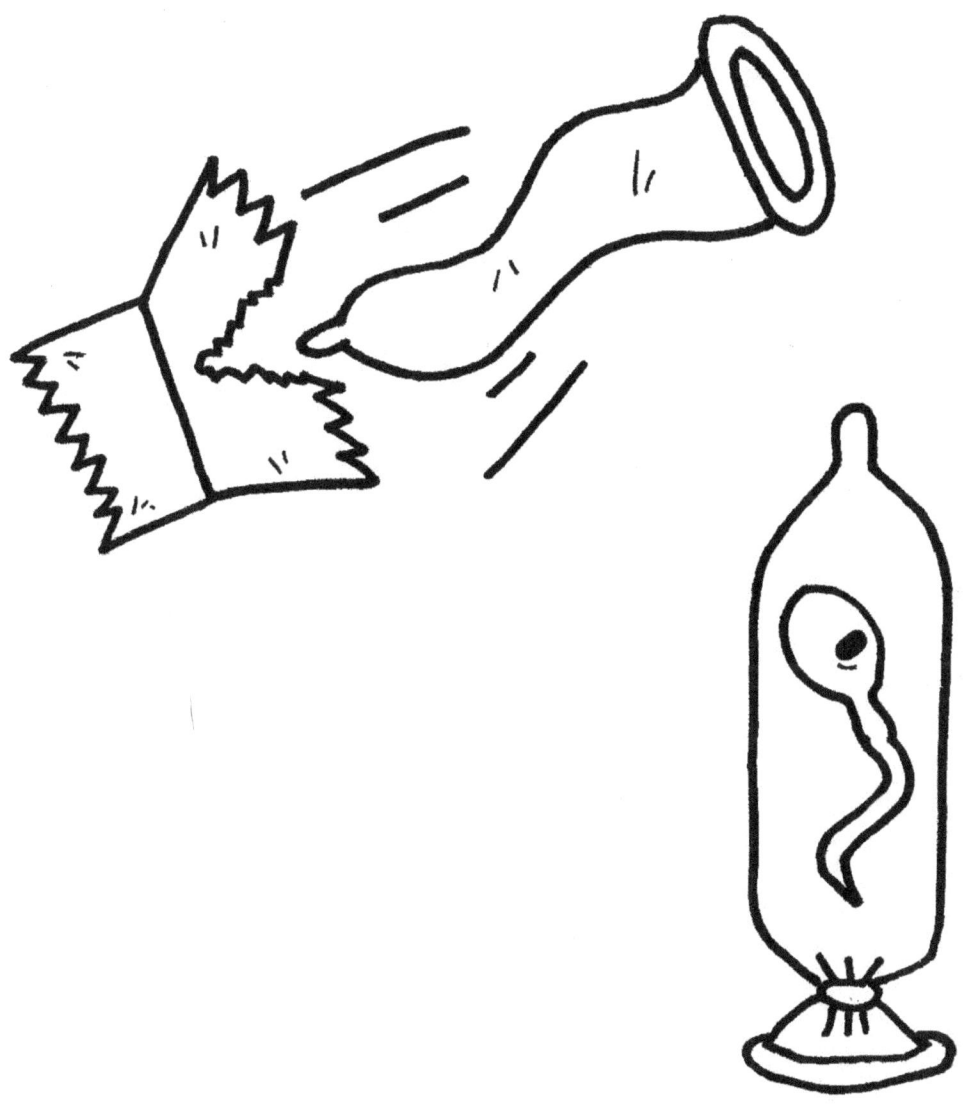

Condomintators

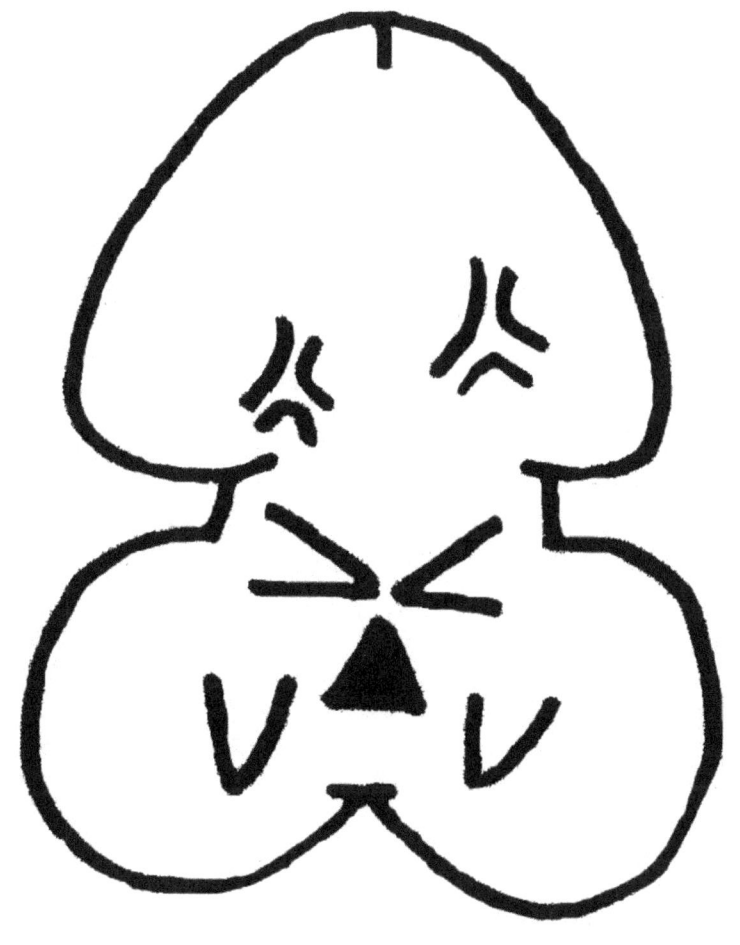

001 Bulbousore

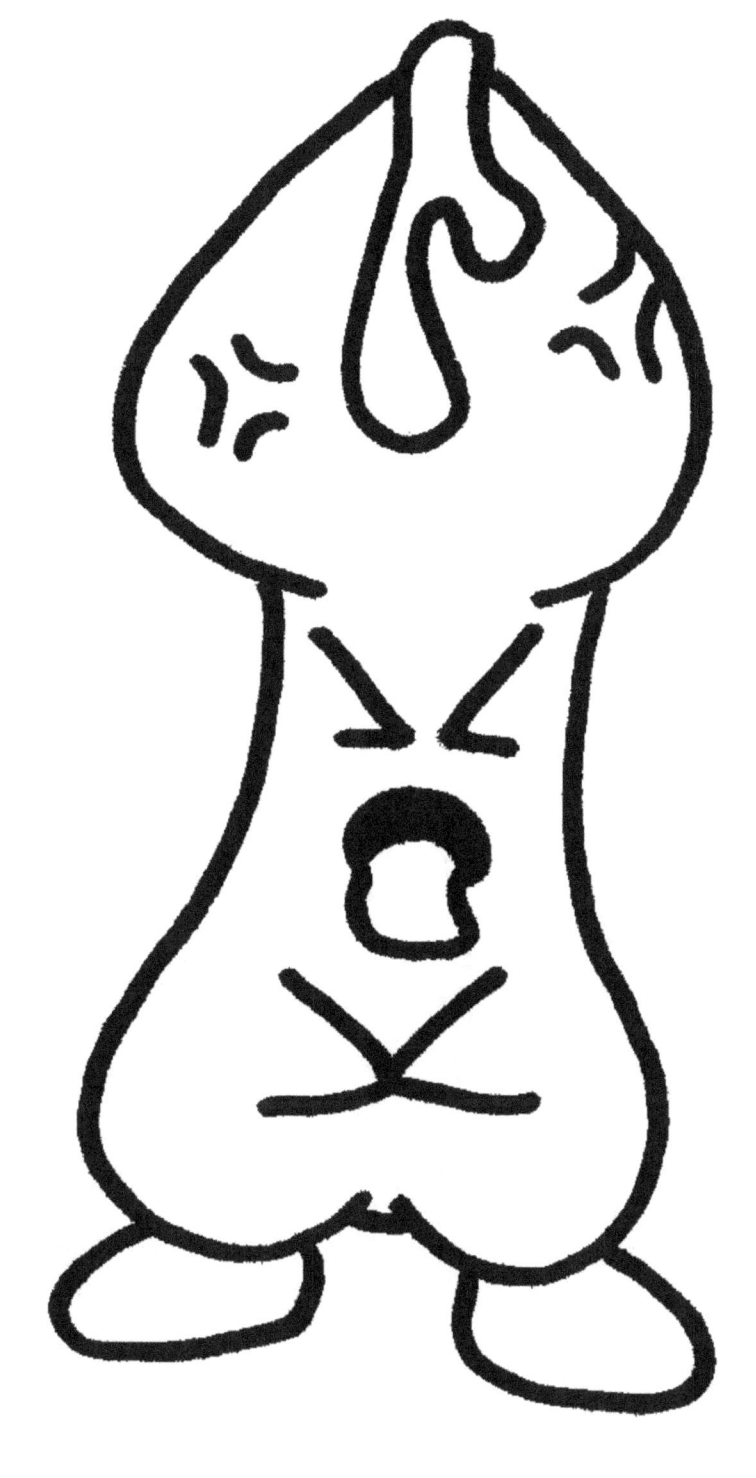

002 Pusore

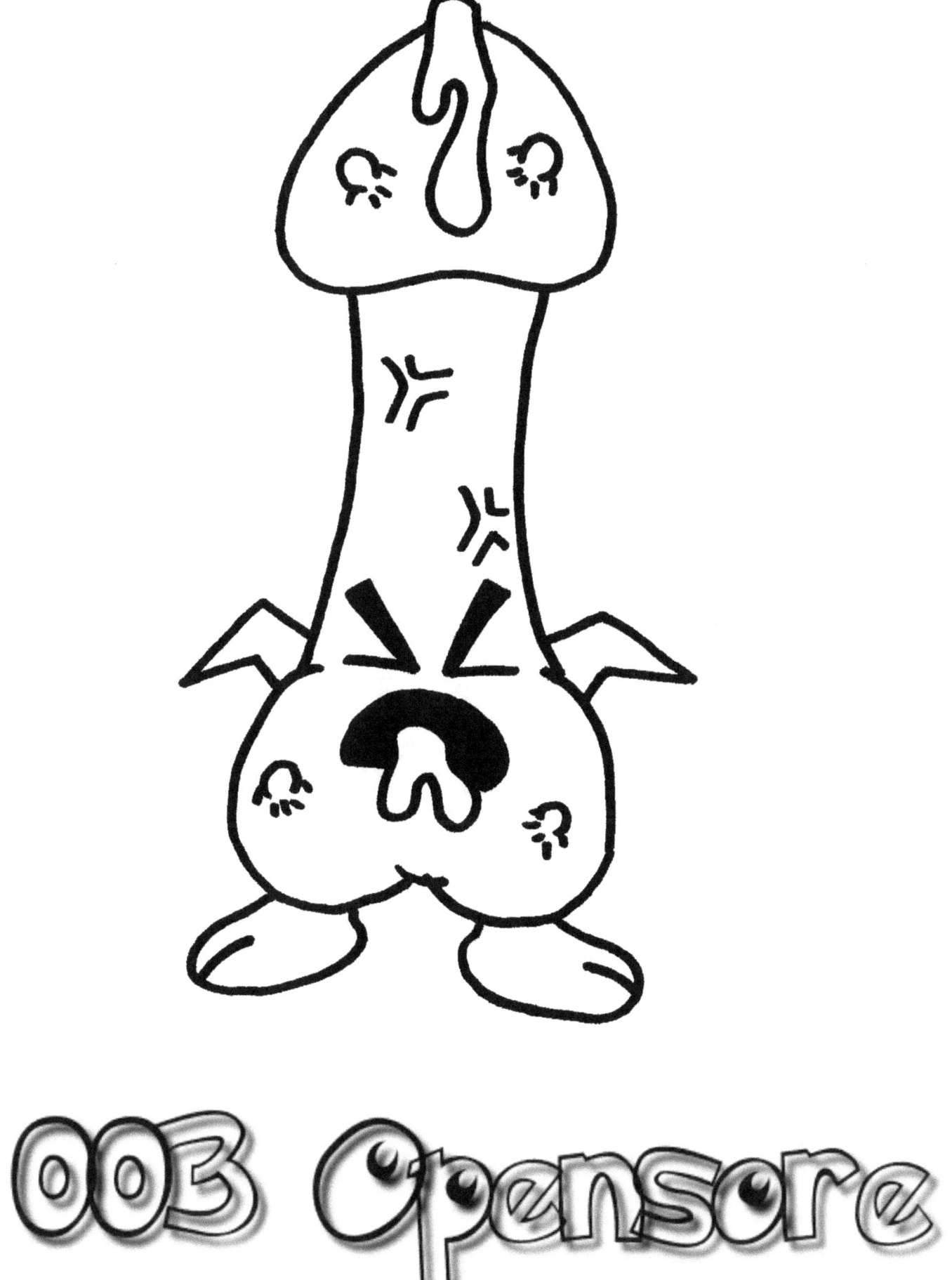

003 Opensore

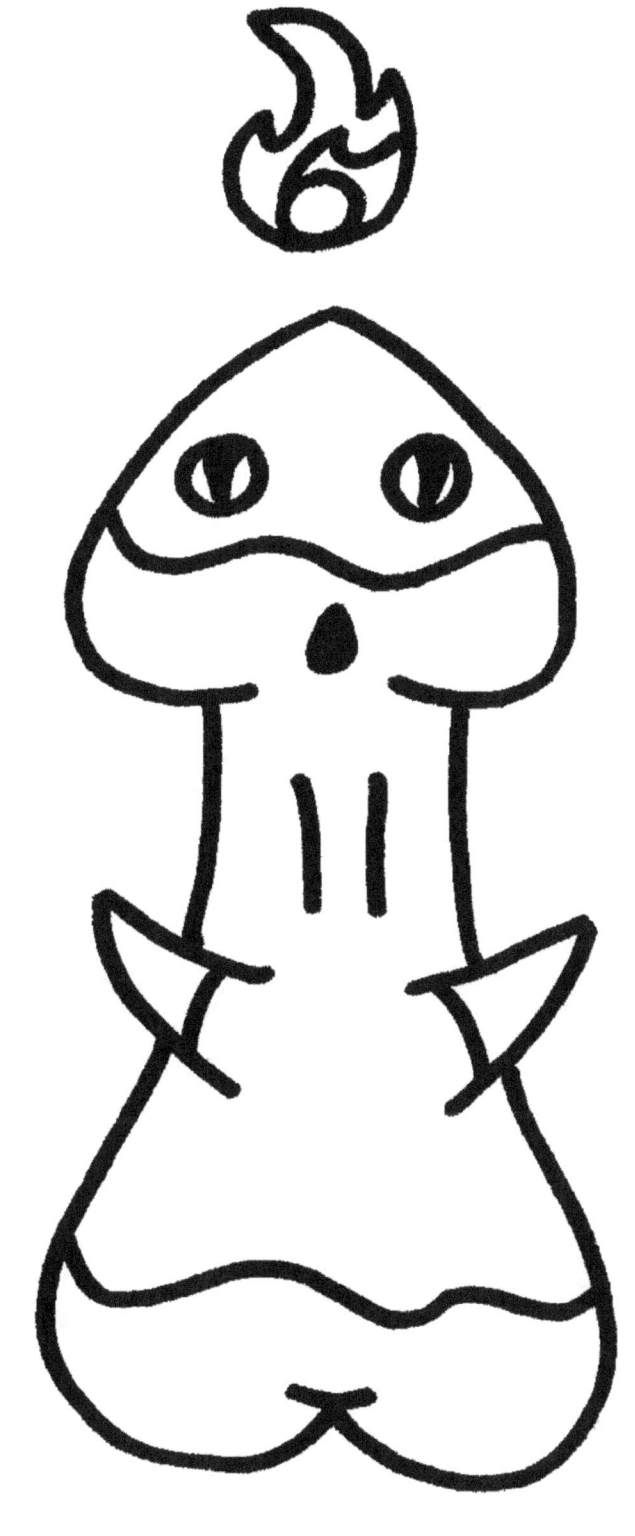

004 Chardmember

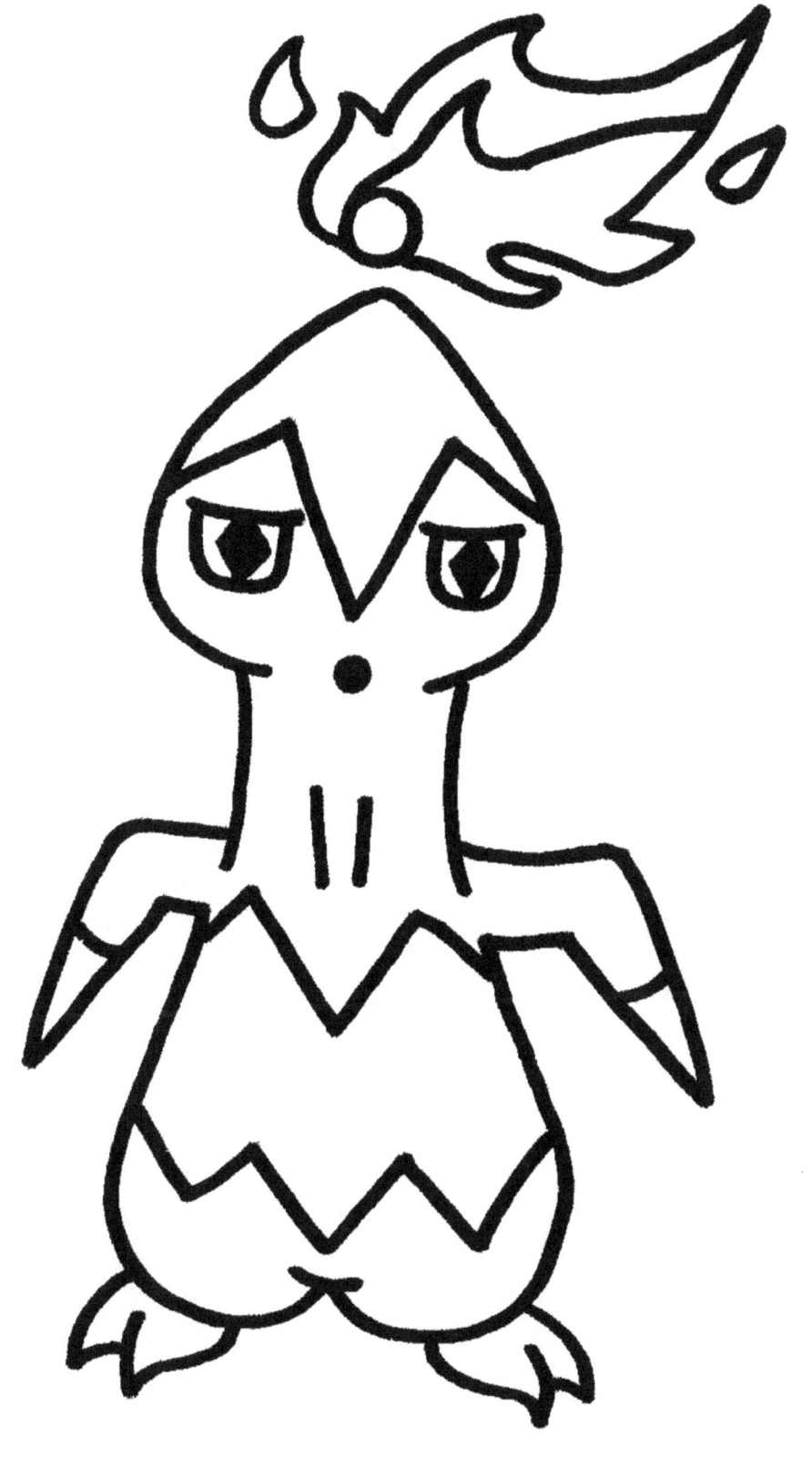

005 Charwacker

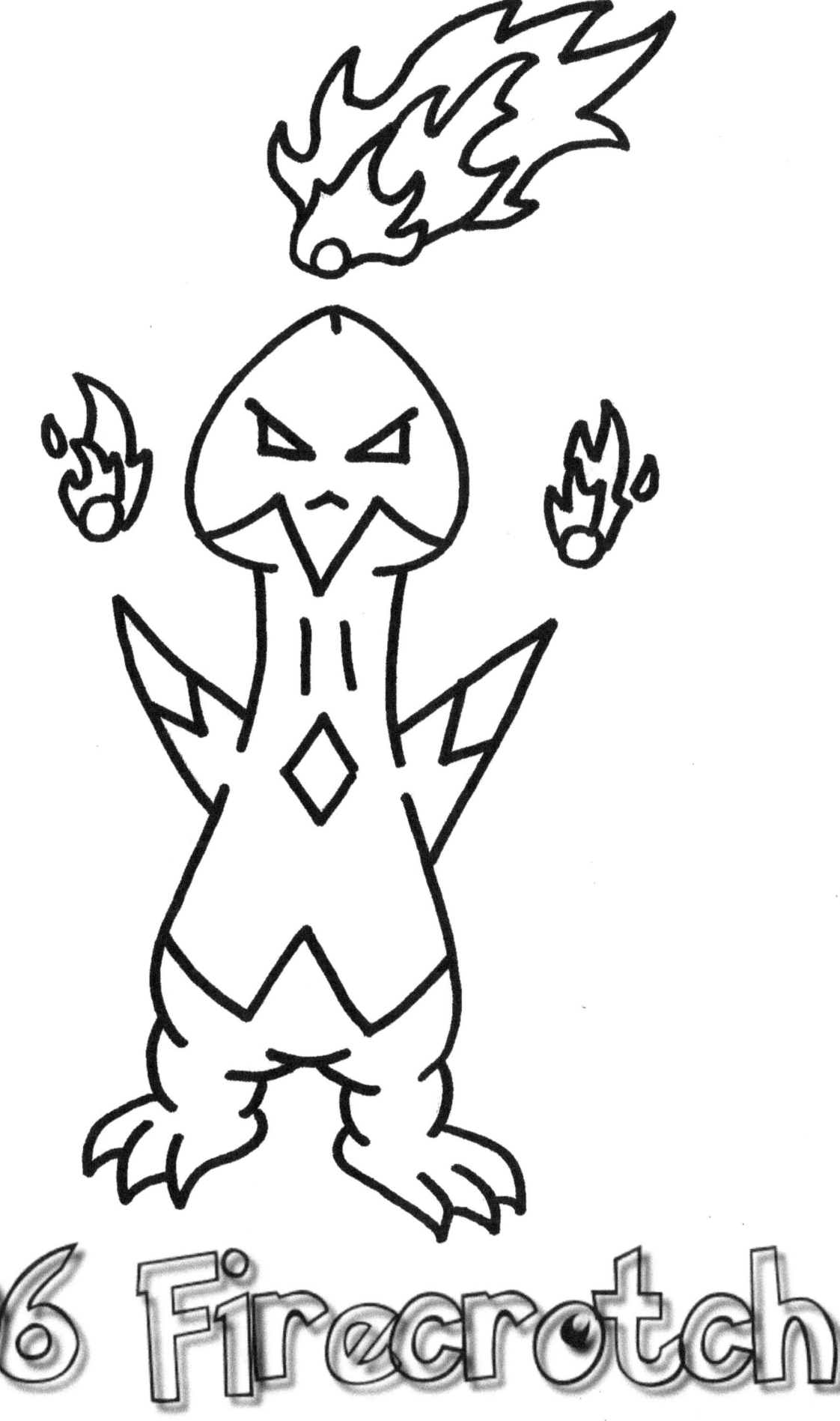

006 Firecrotch

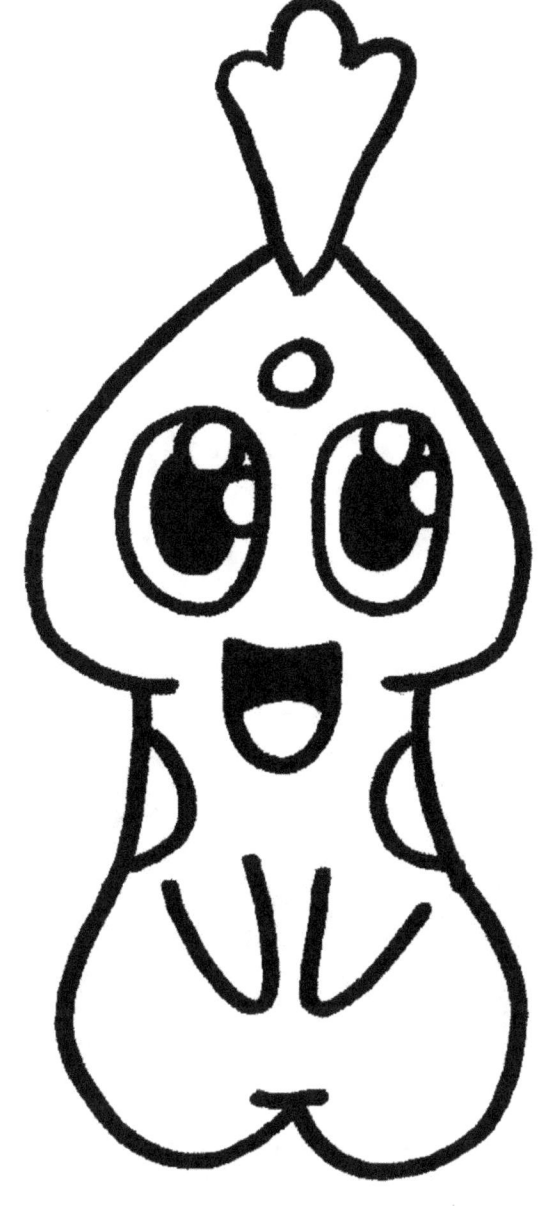

007 Squirter

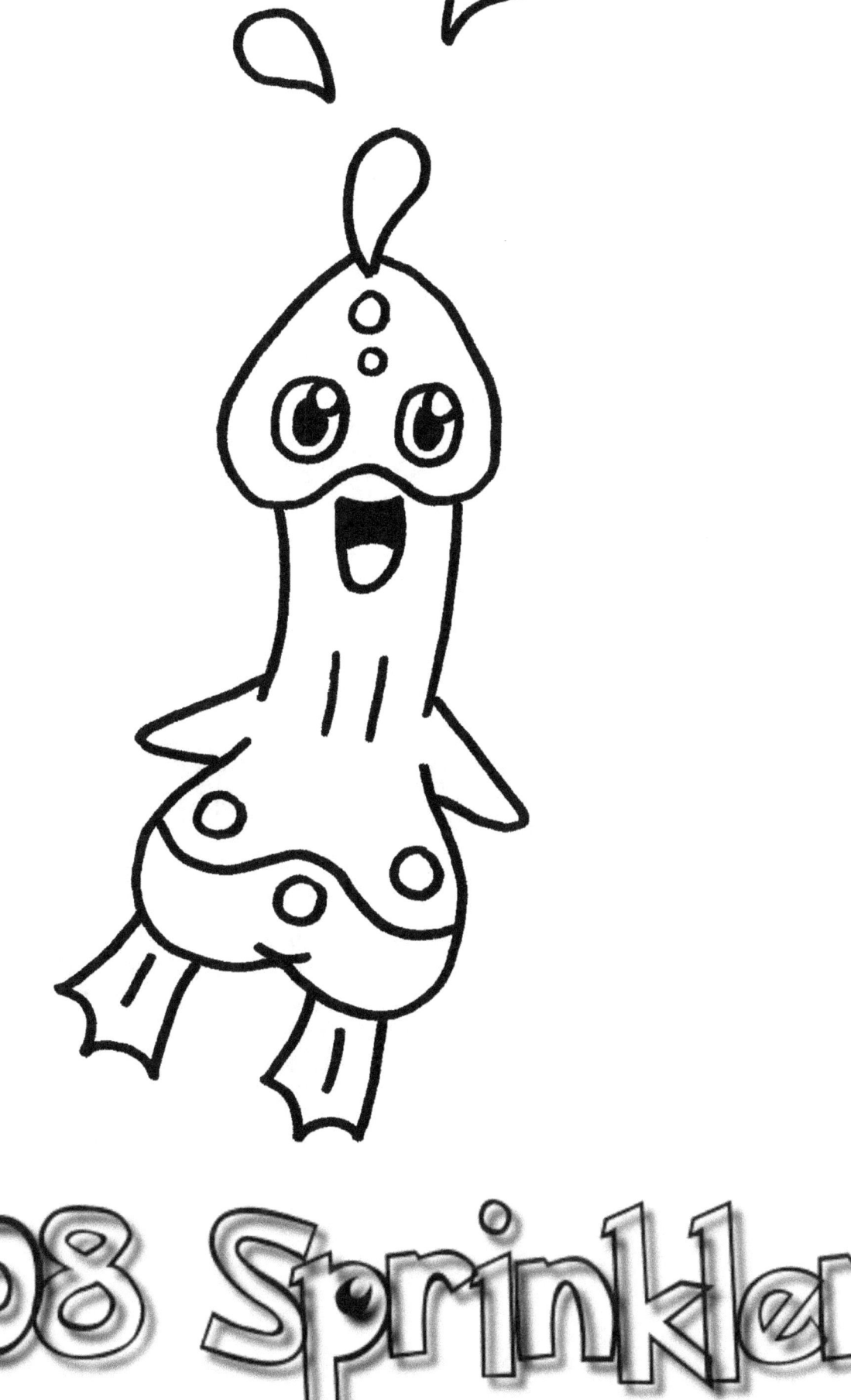

008 Sprinkler

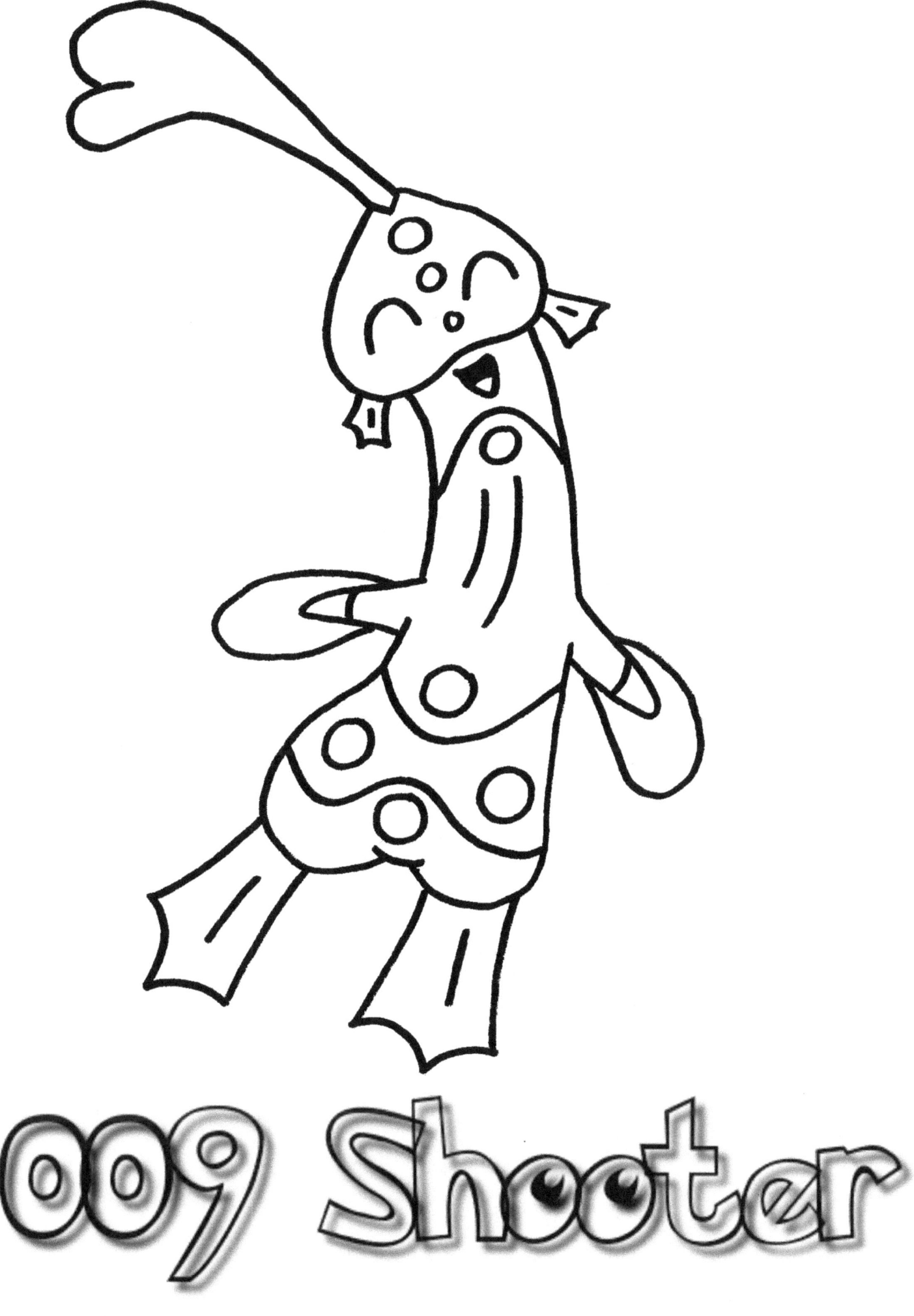

009 Shooter

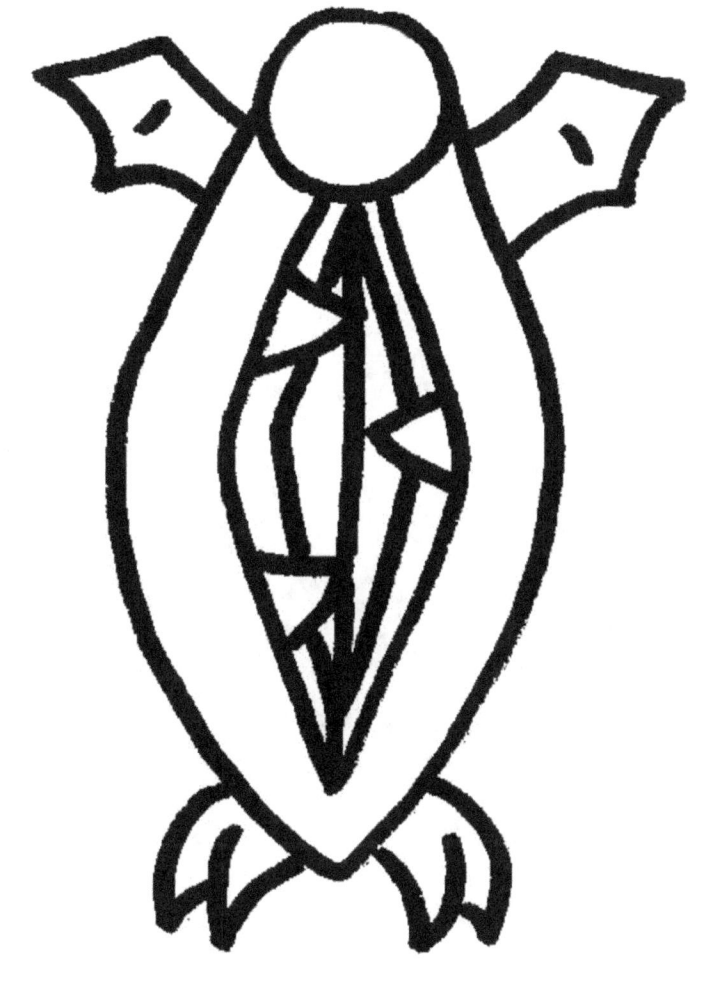

010 Vaginadente

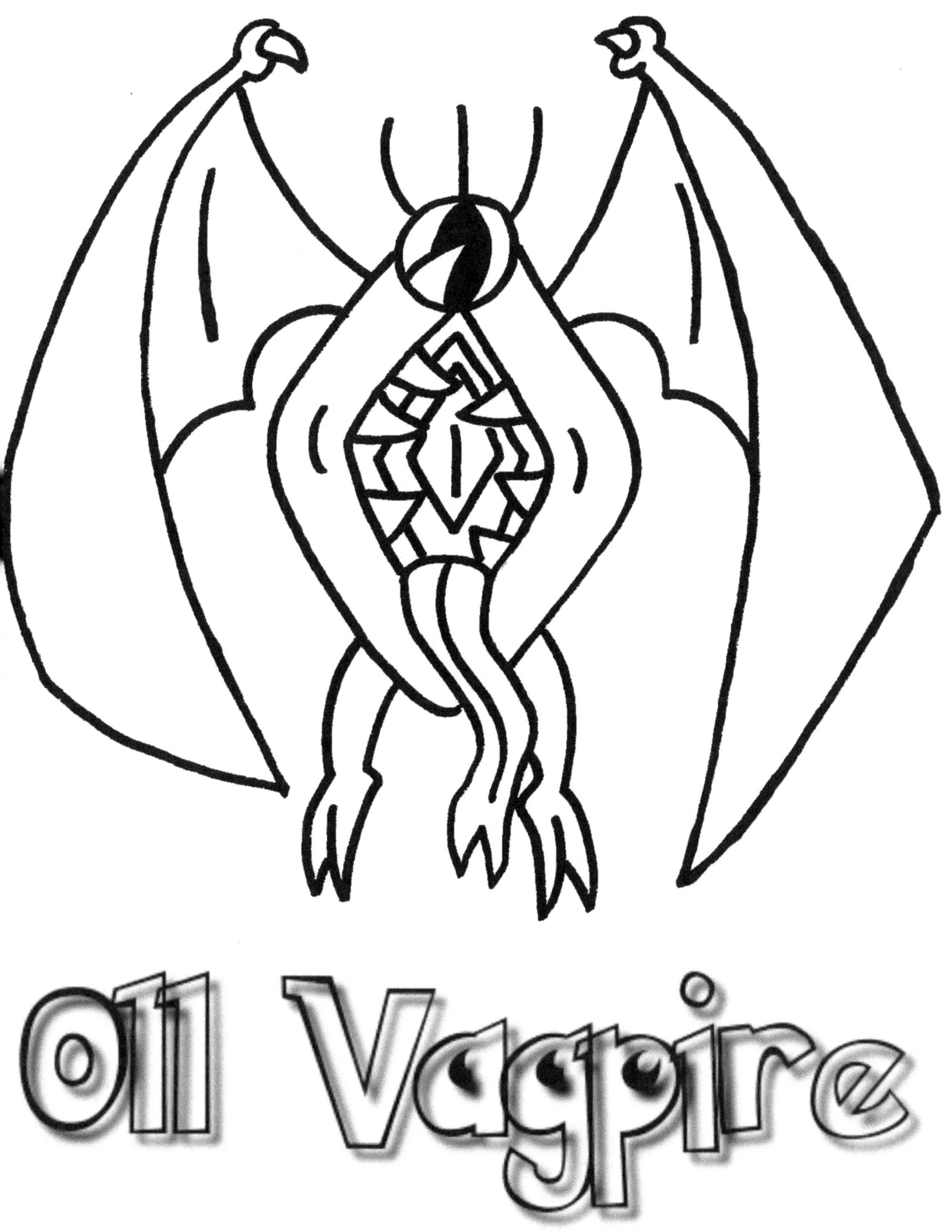

011 Vagpire

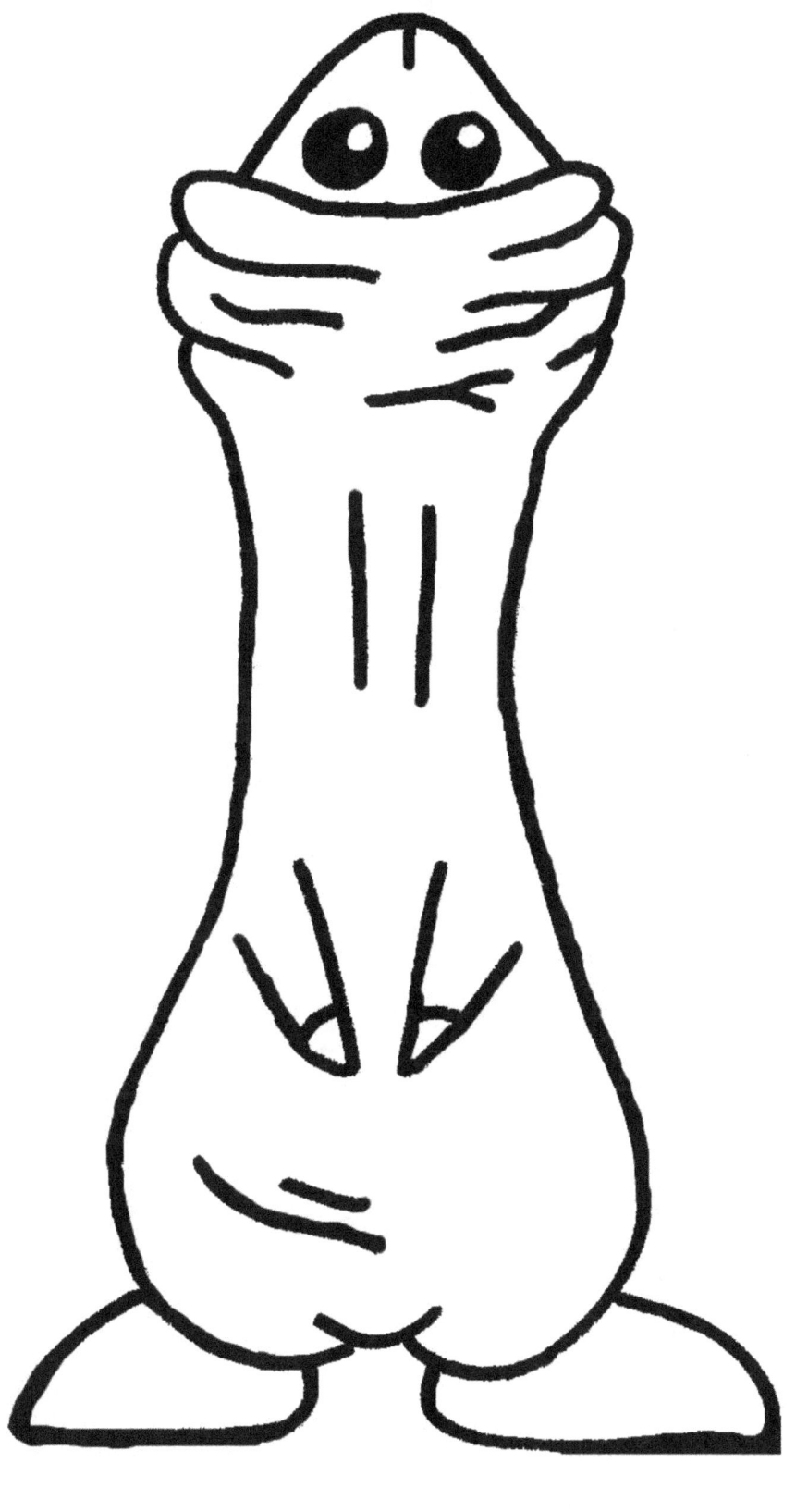

012 Turtleneck

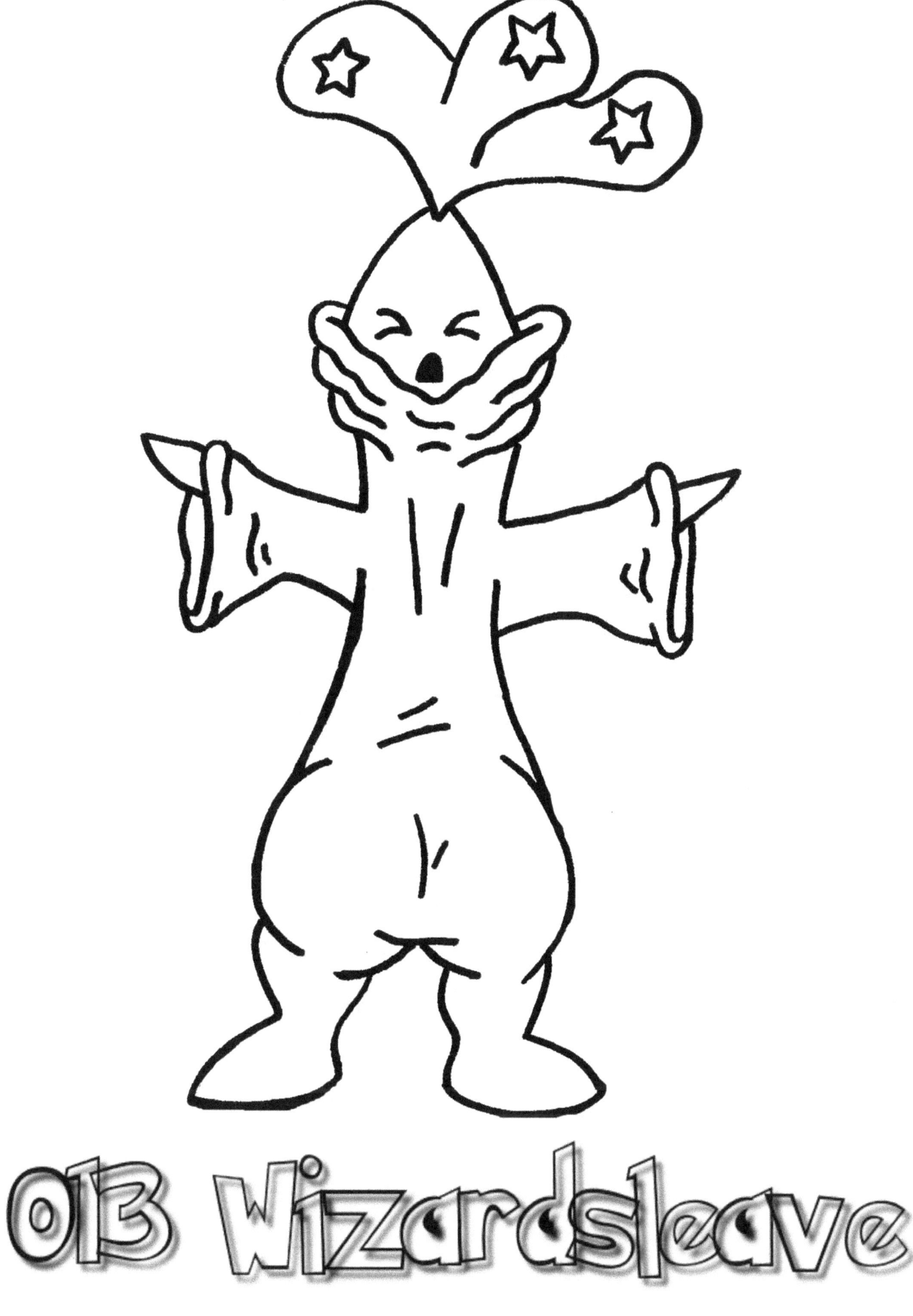

013 Wizardsleave

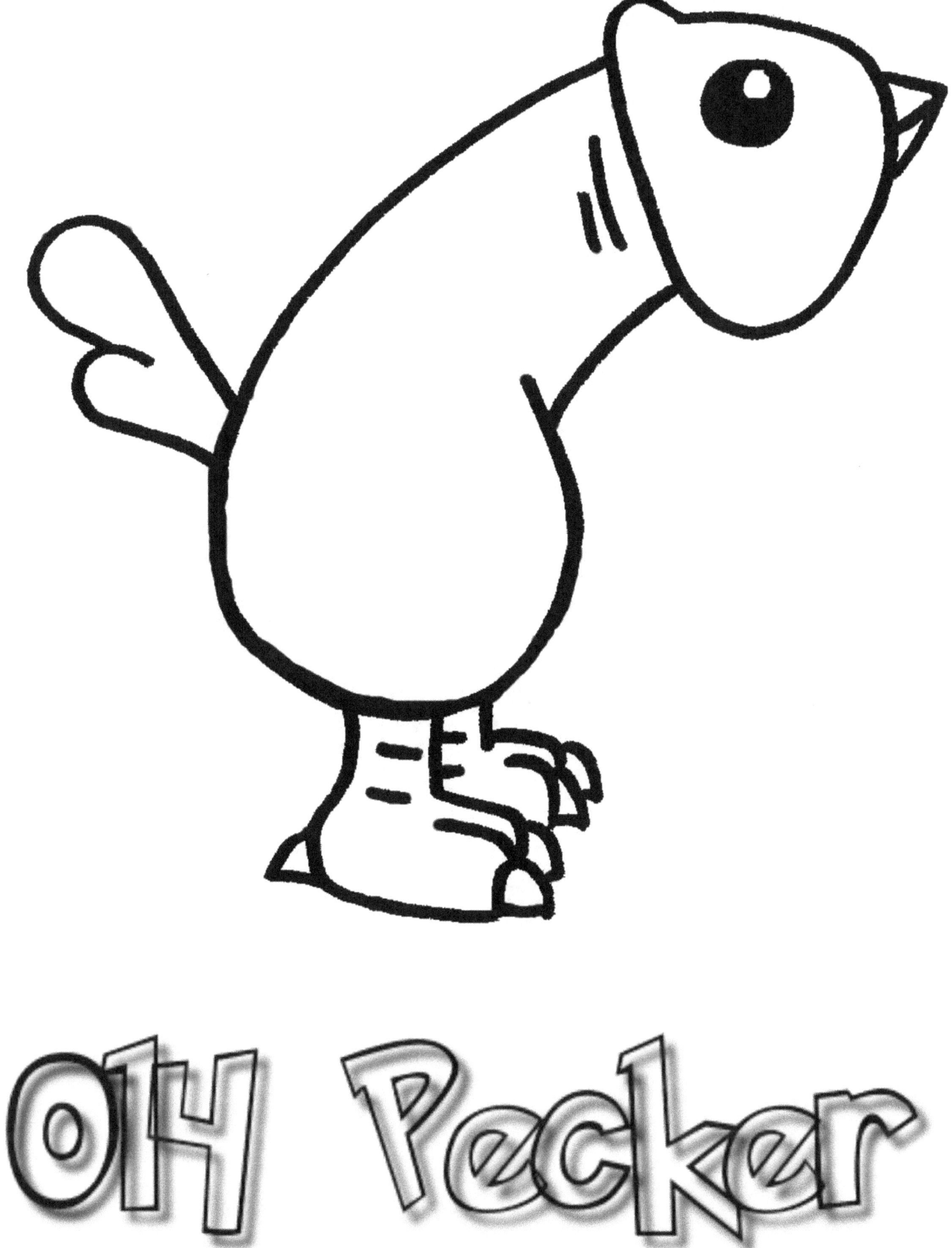

014 Pecker

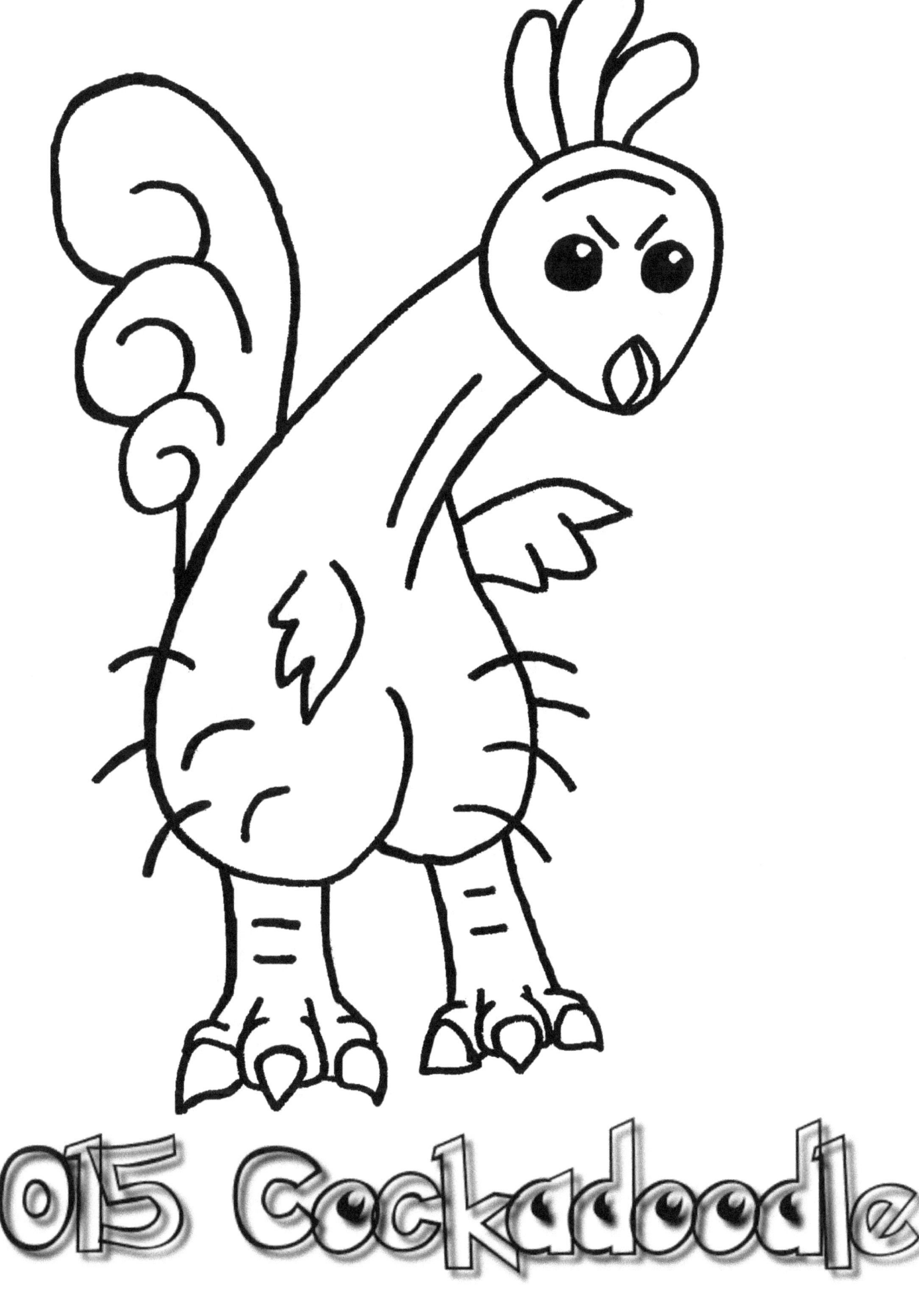

015 Cockadoodle

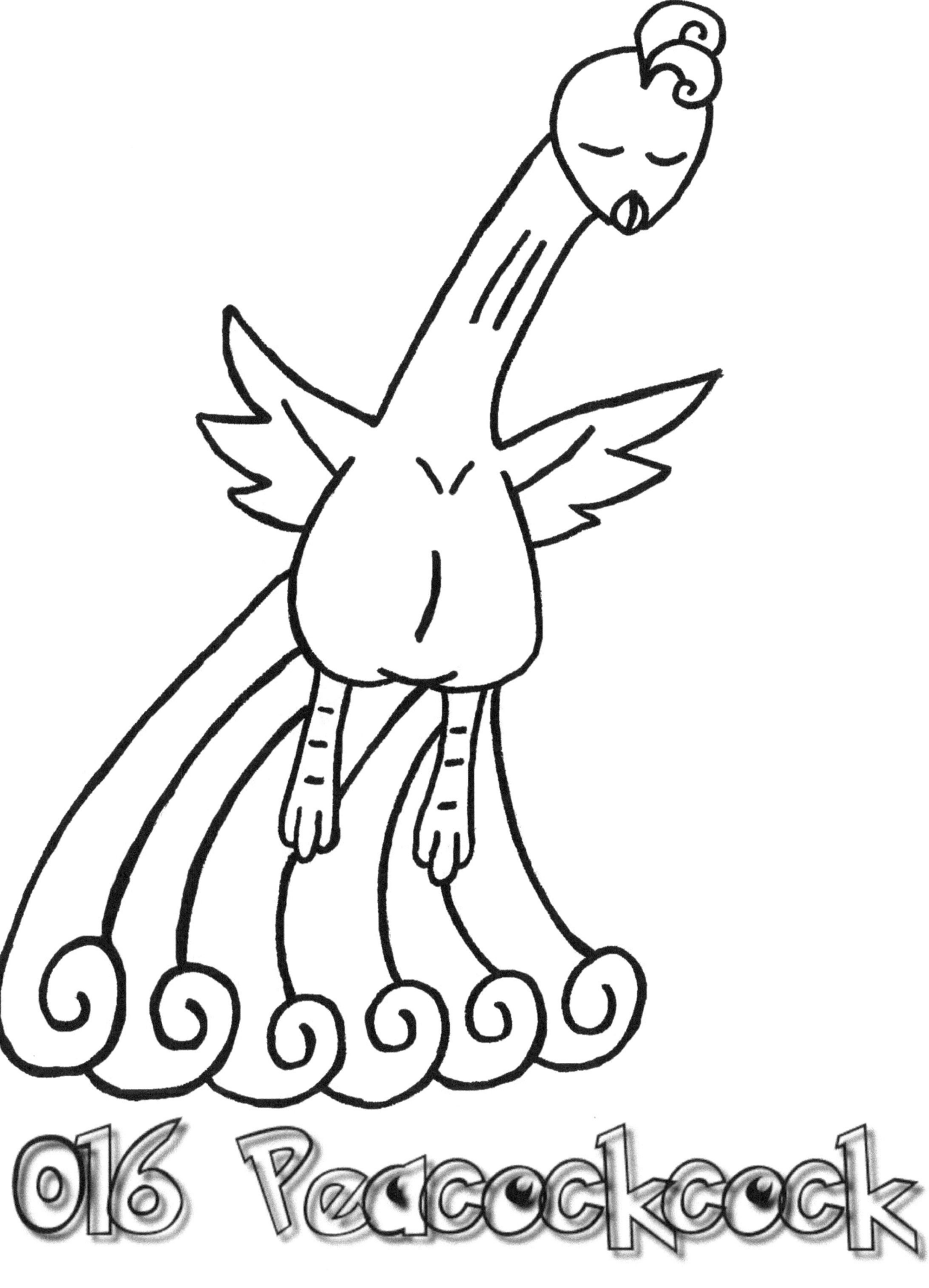

016 Peacockcock

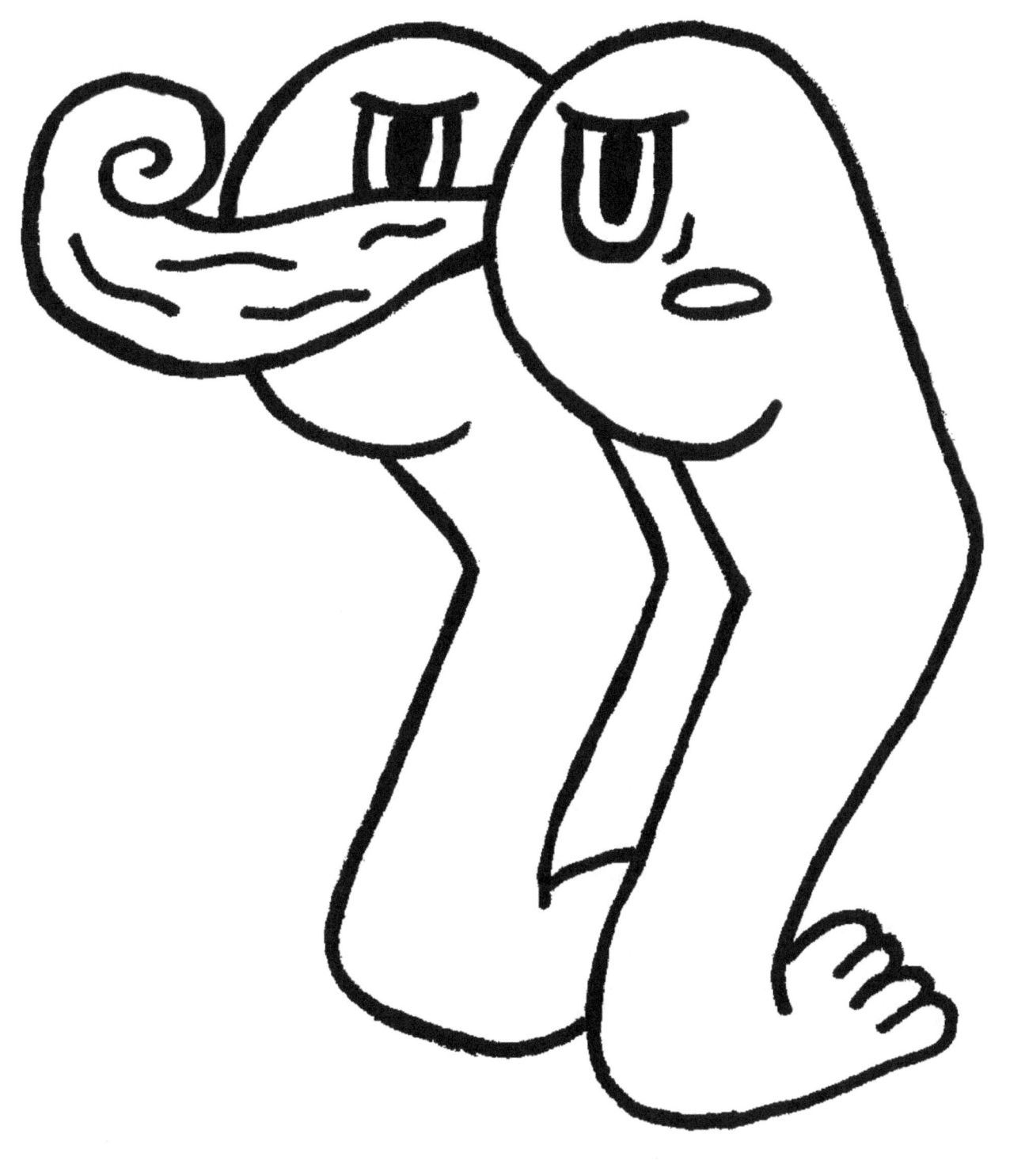

017 Windbreaker

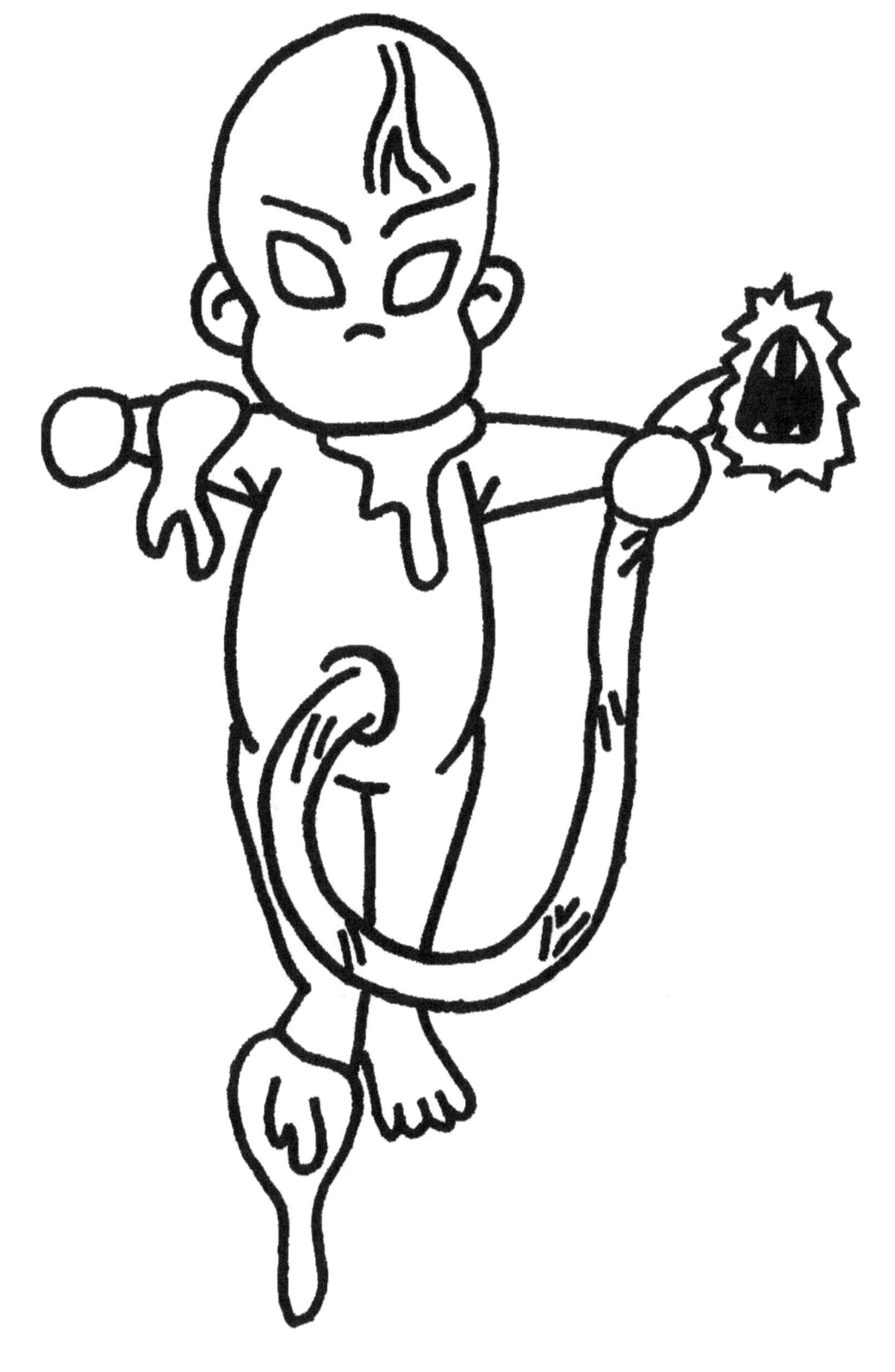

018 Defeatus

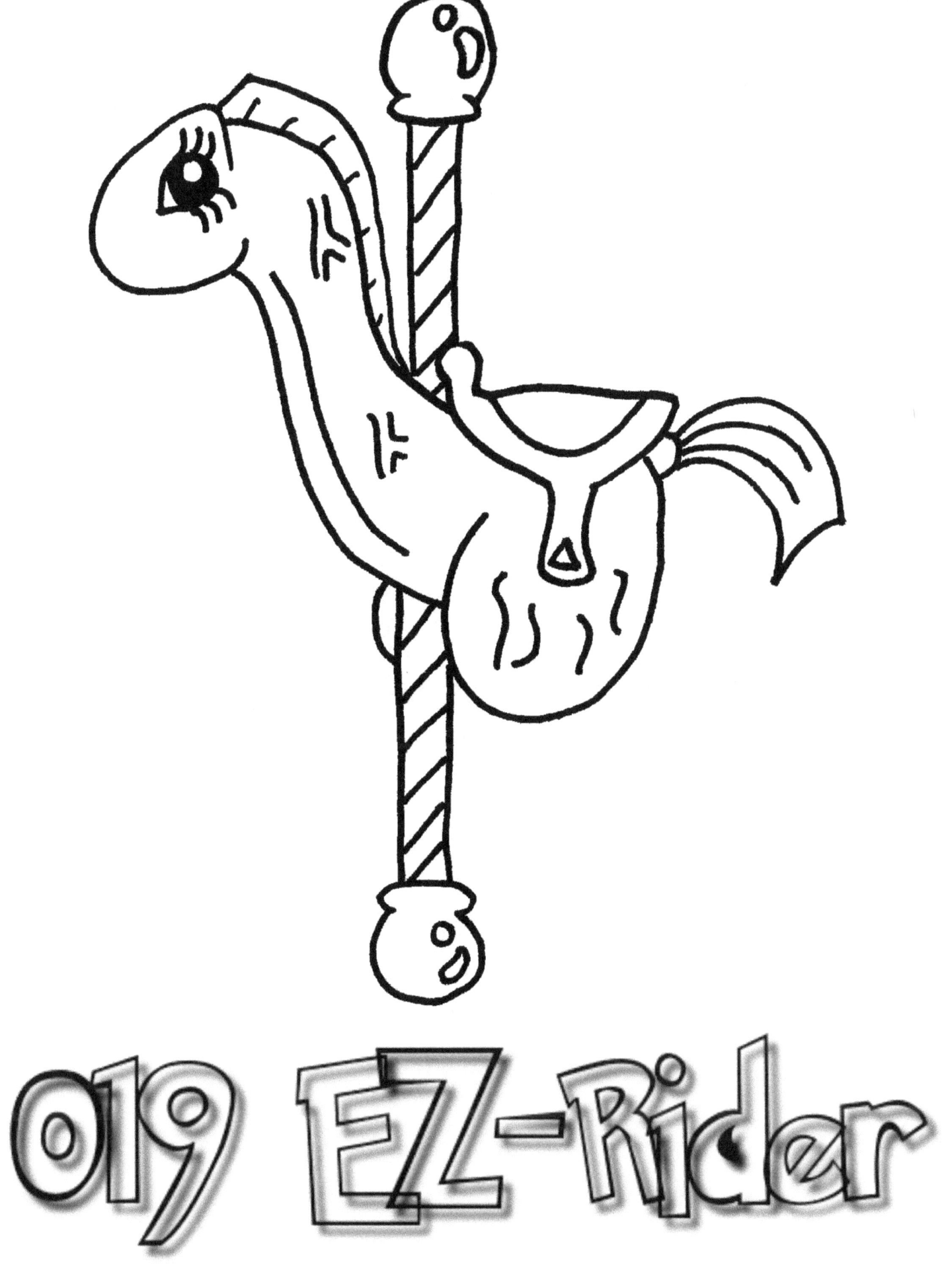

019 EZ-Rider

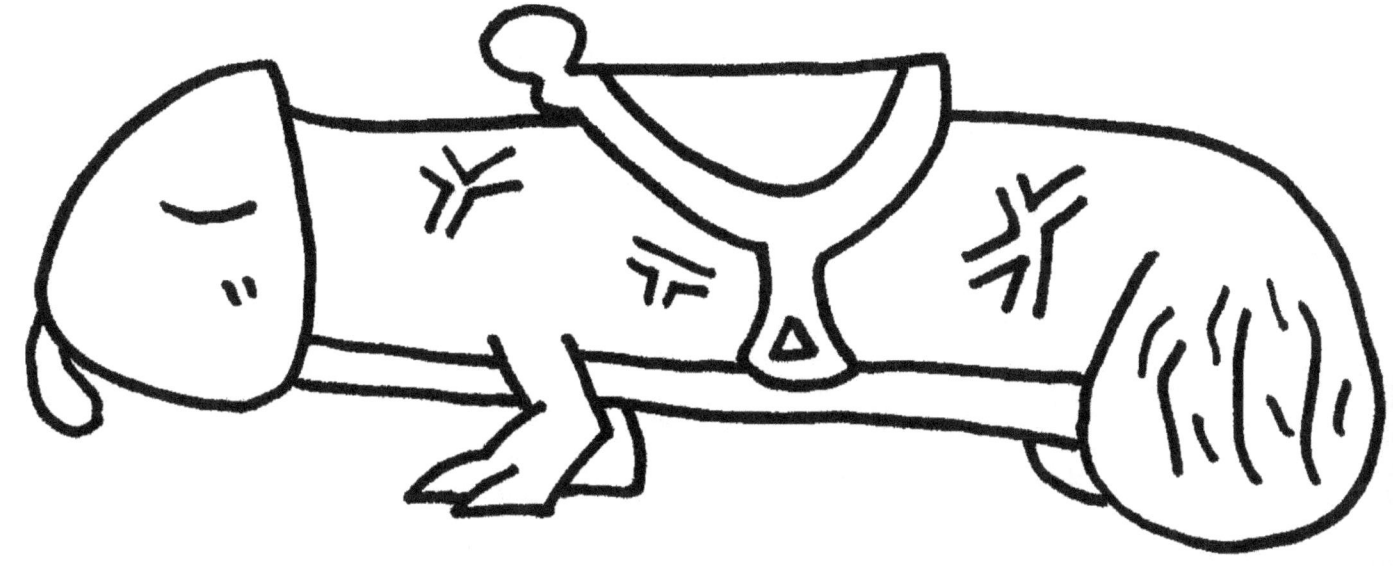

020 Low-Rider

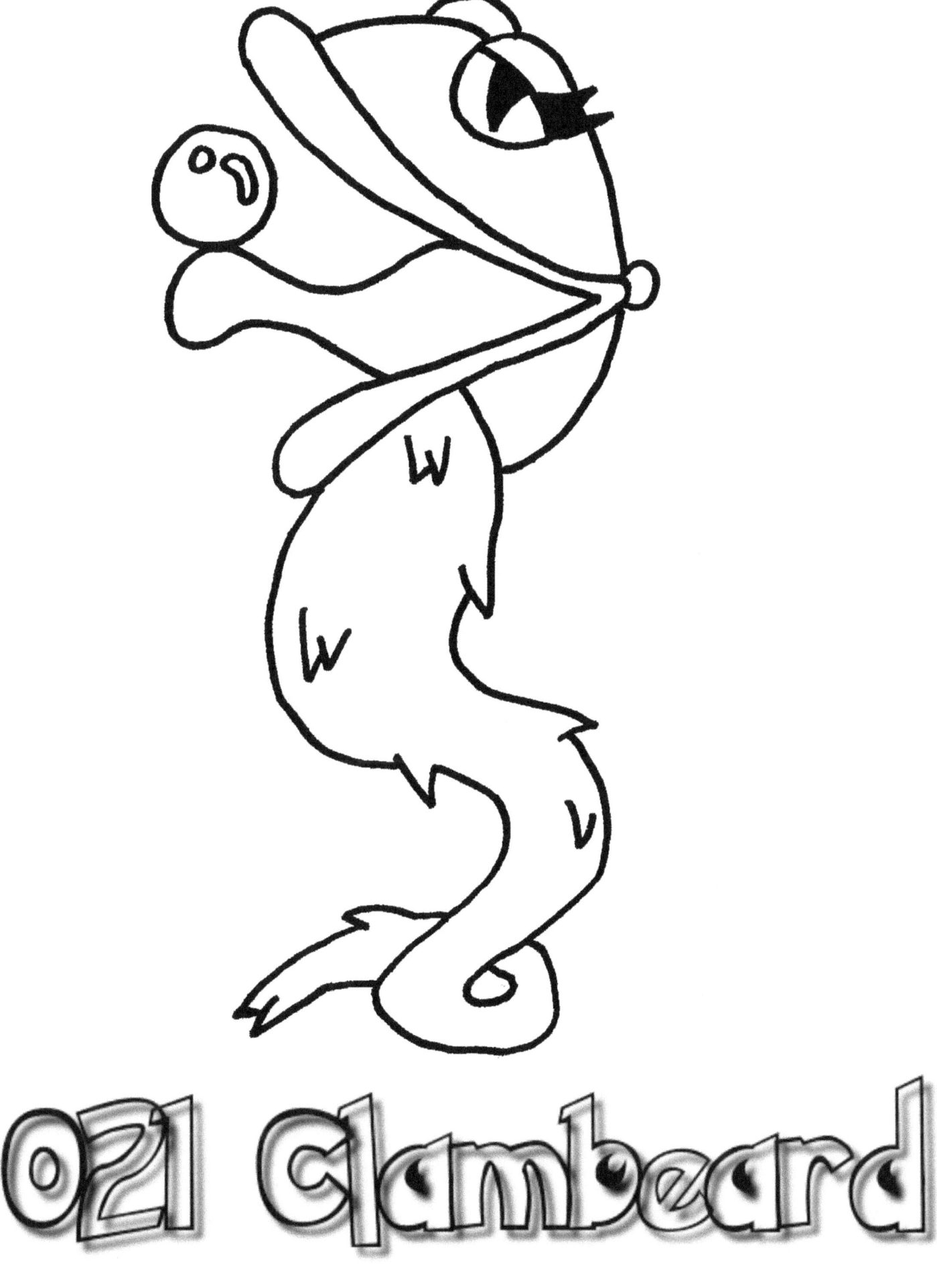

021 Clambeard

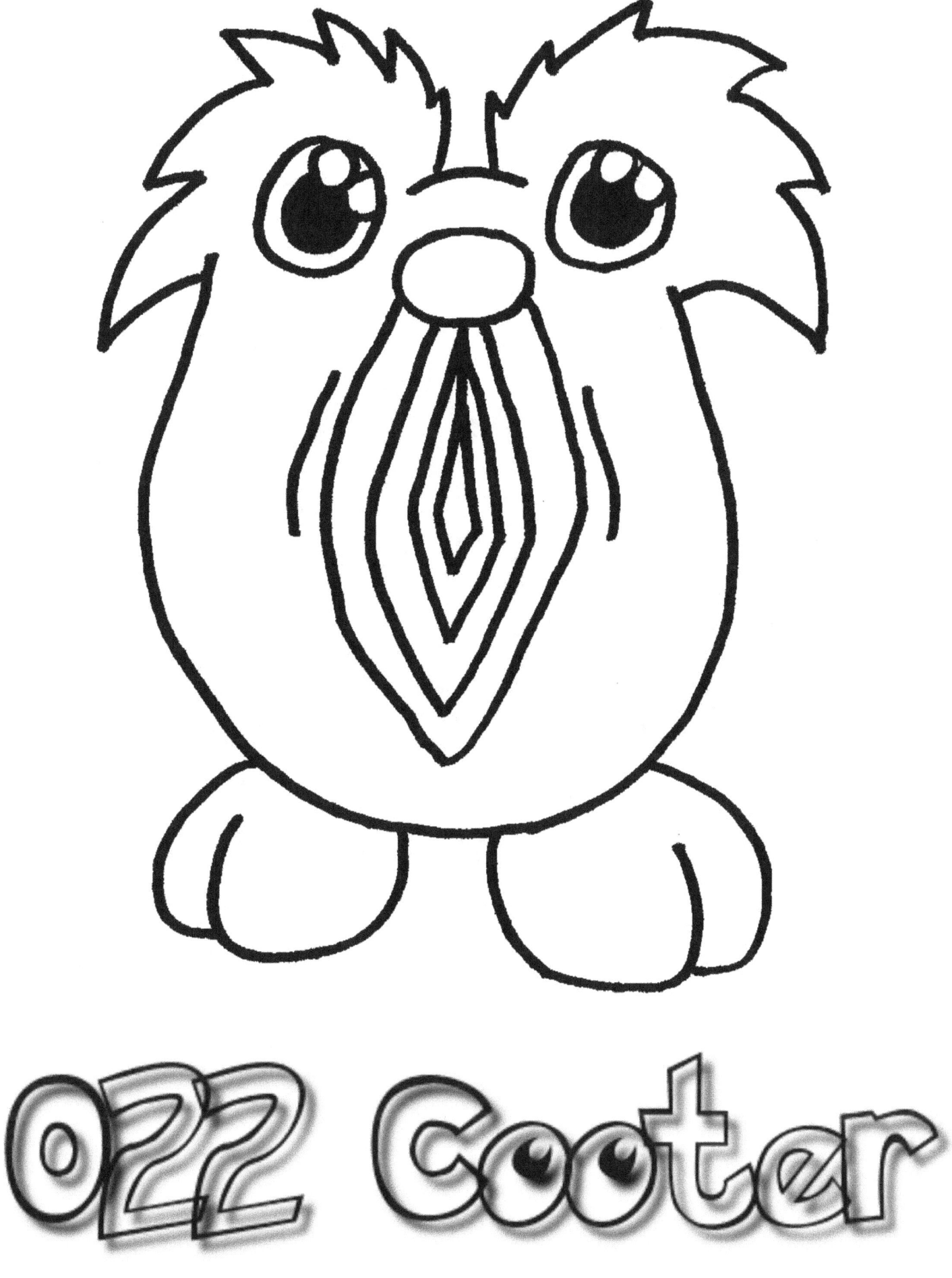

022 Cooter

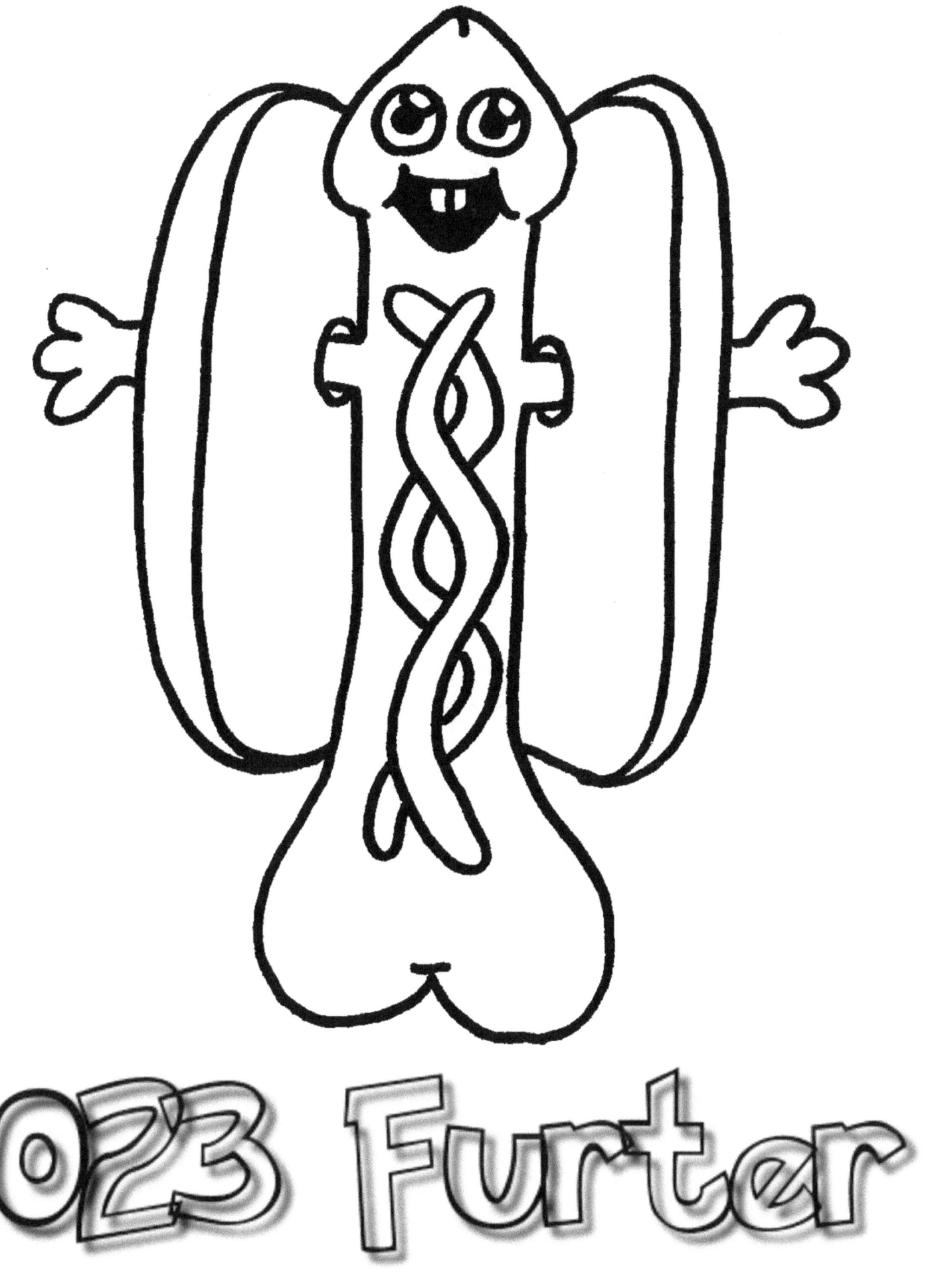

023 Furter

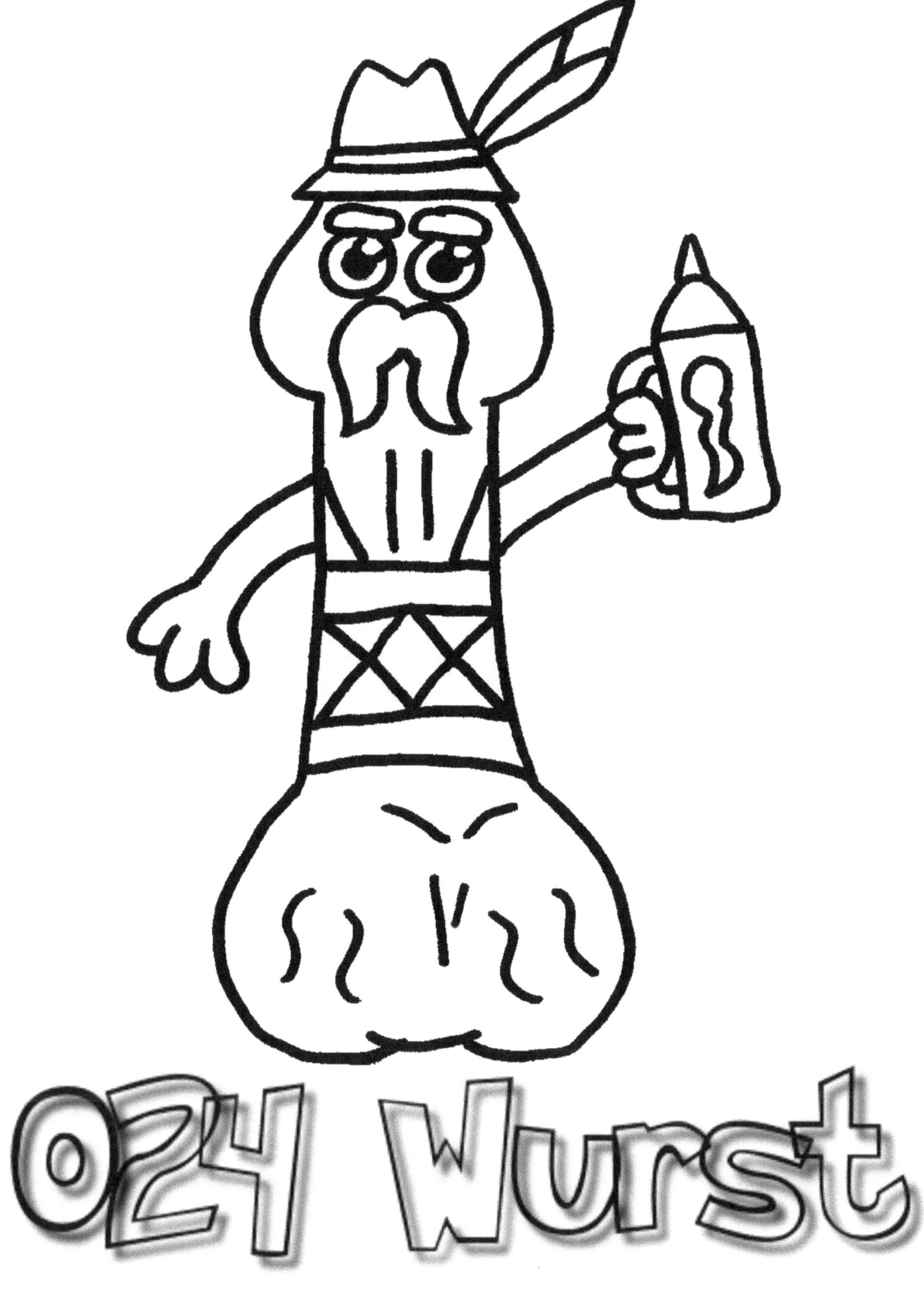

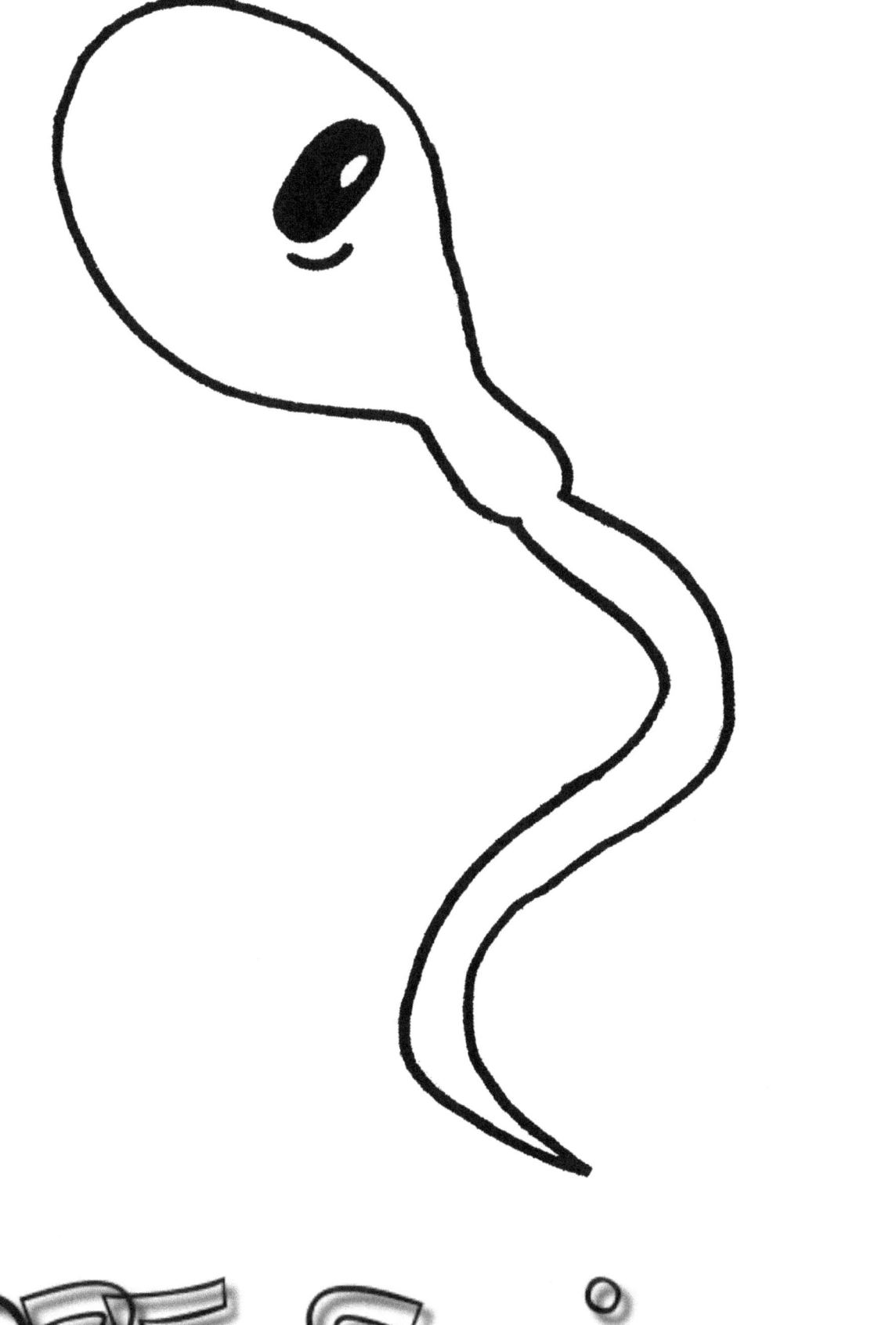

025 Swimma

026 Spludga

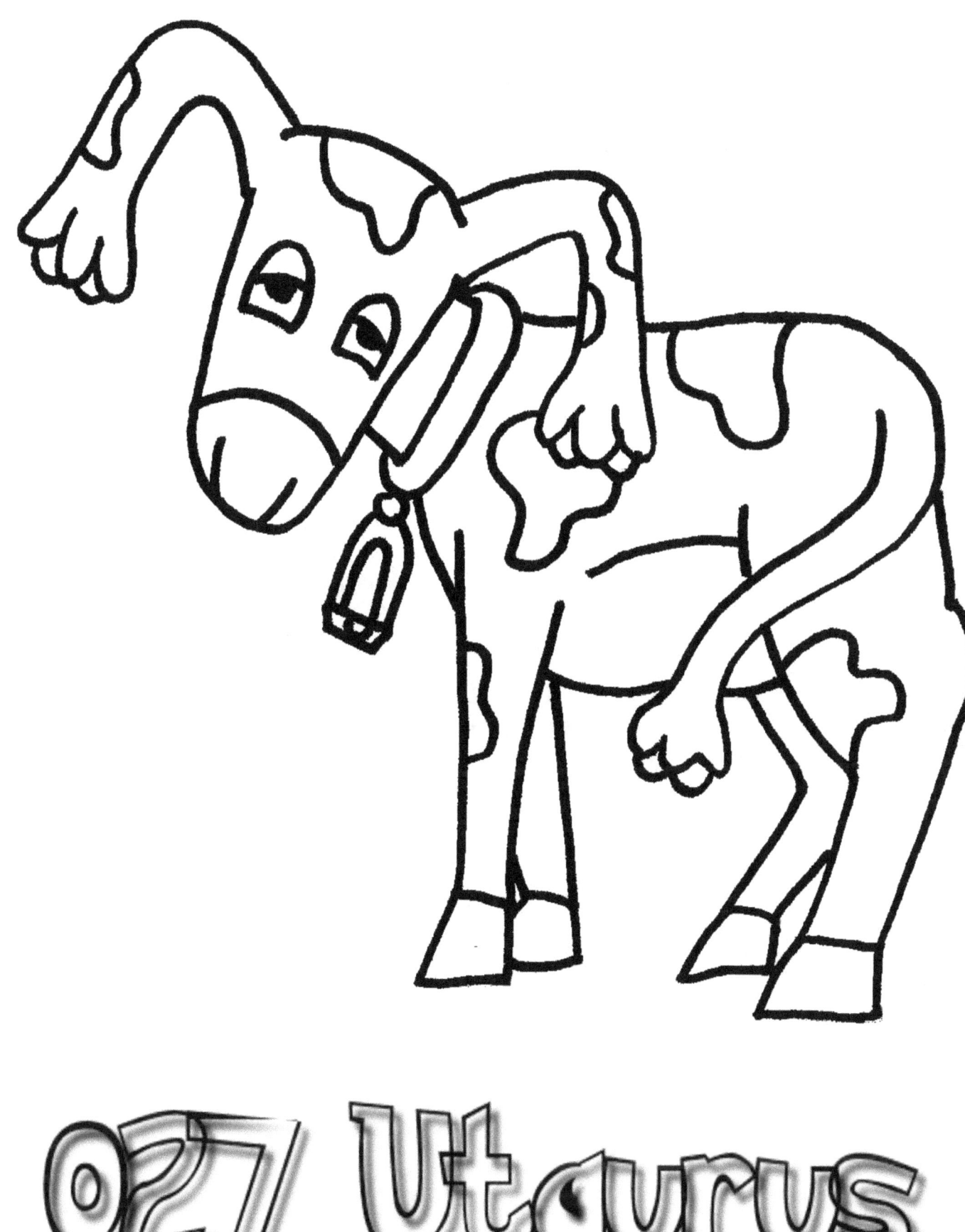

027 Utaurus

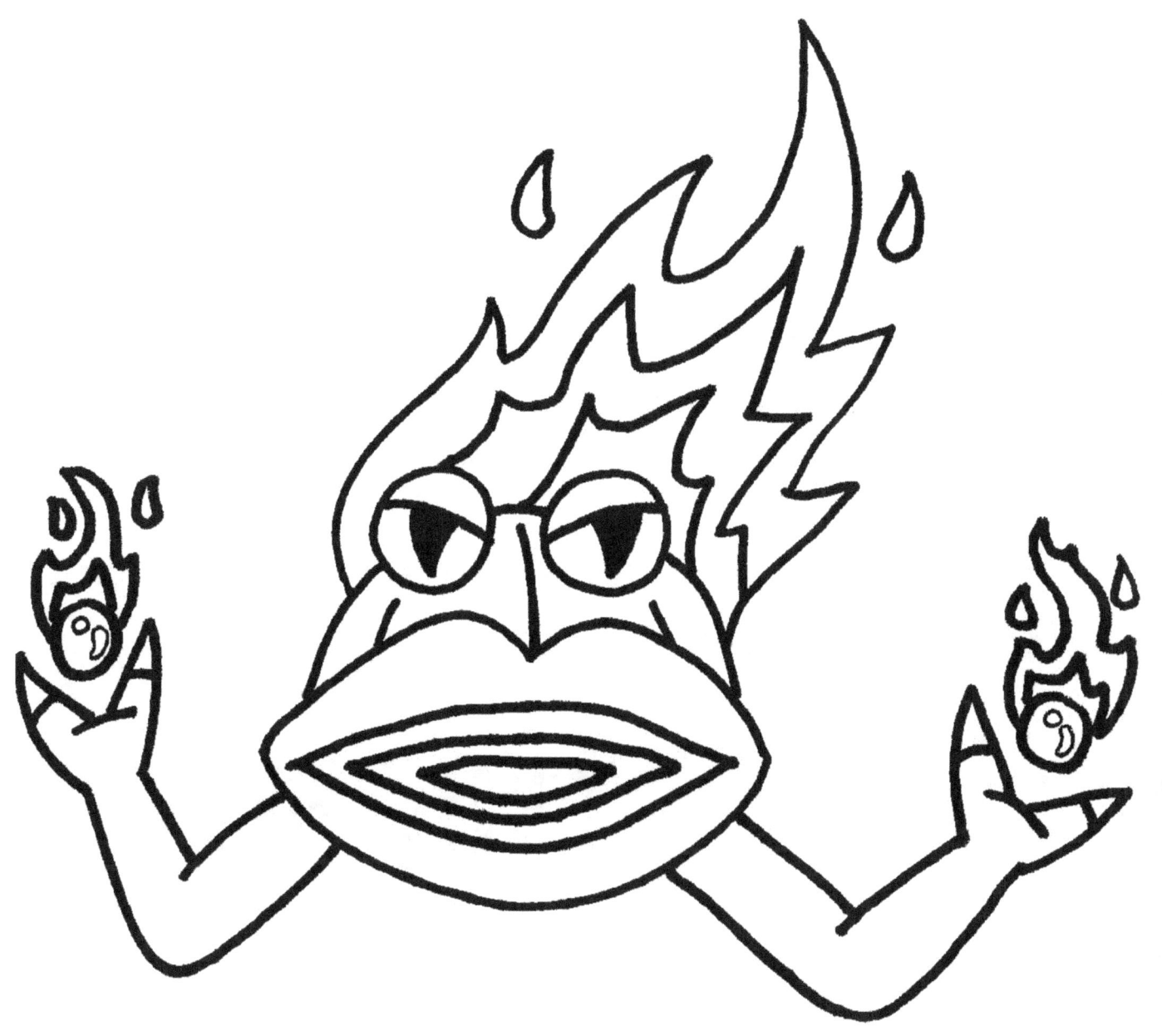

028 Clamydia

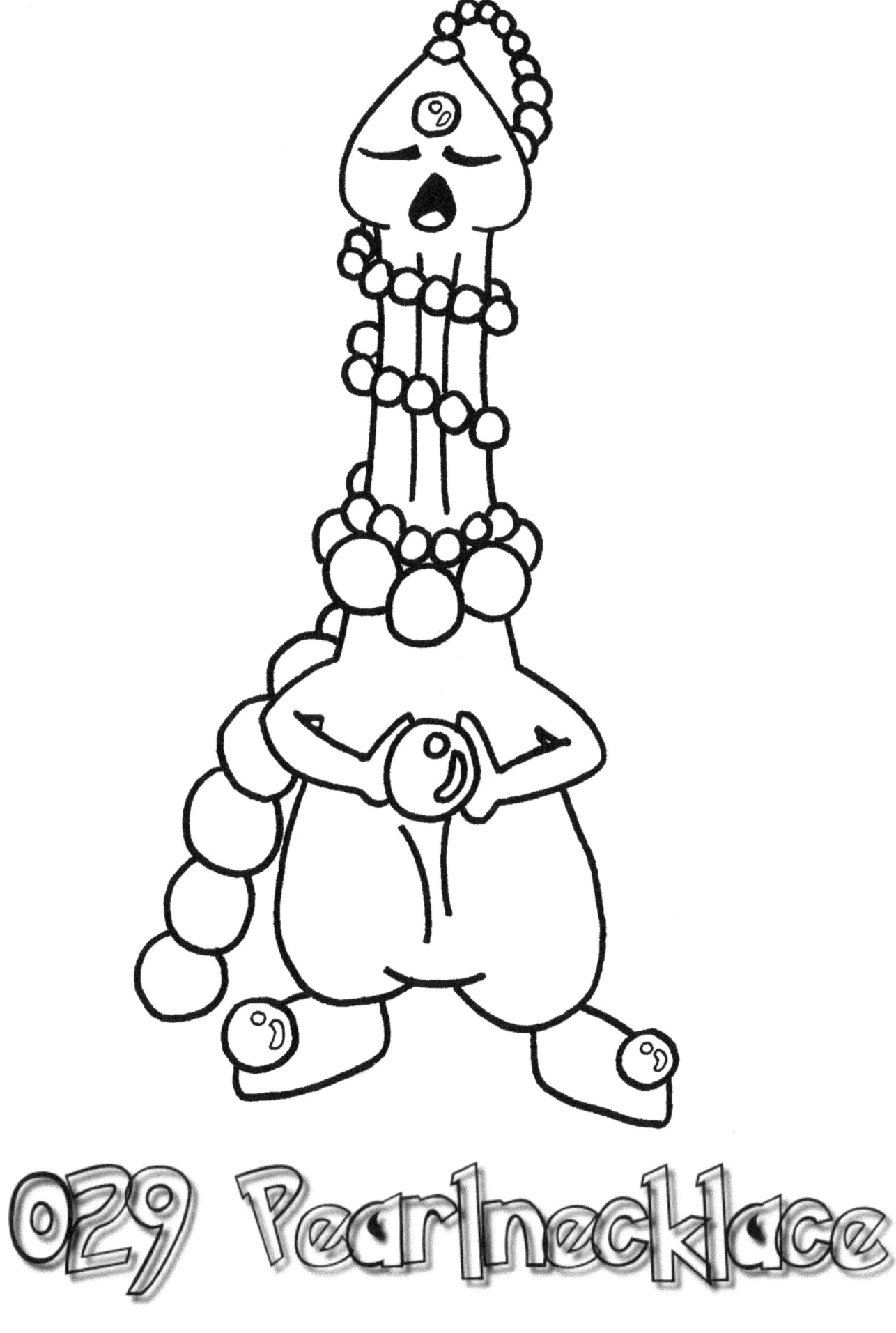

029 Pearlnecklace

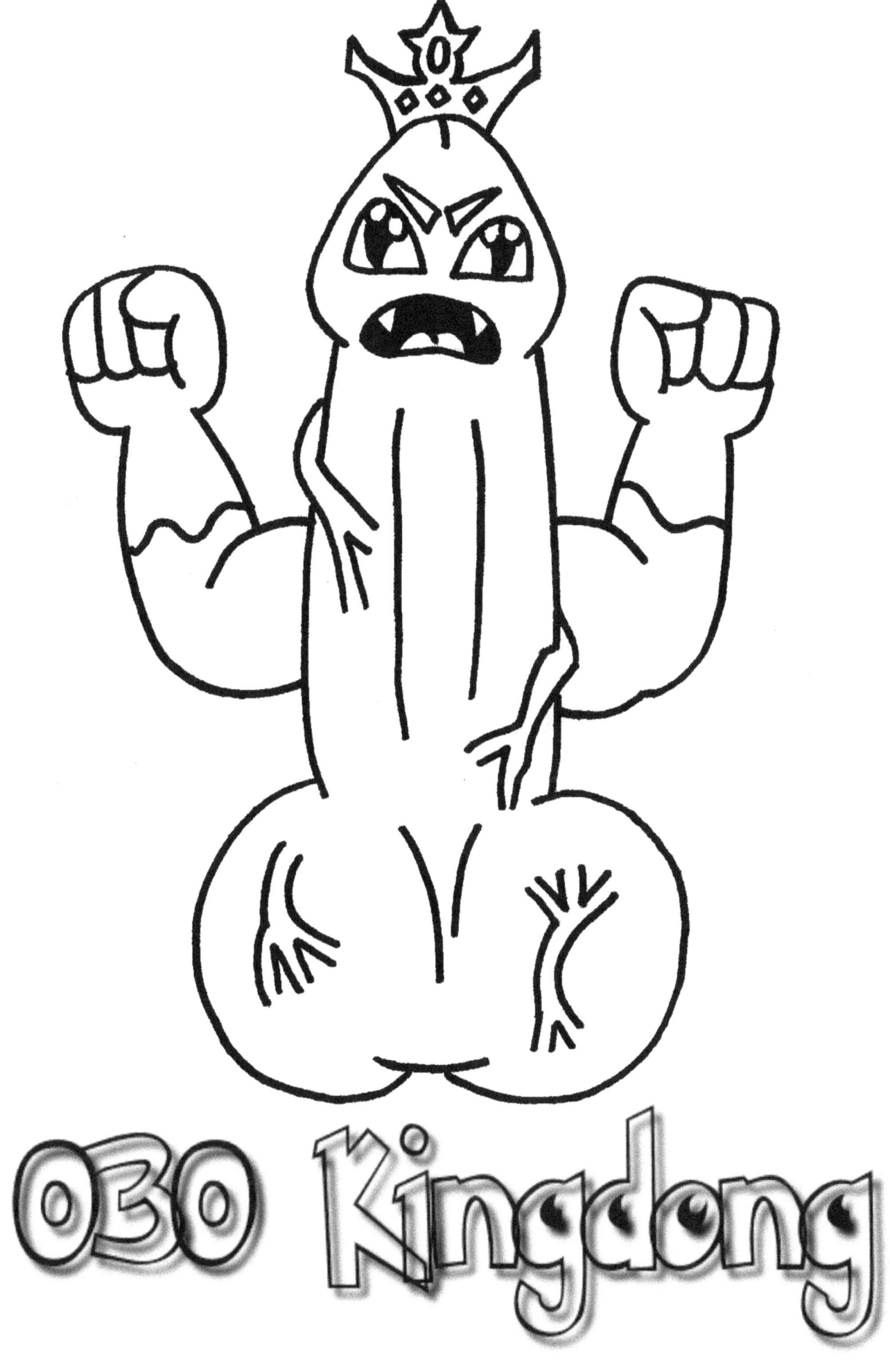

030 Kingdong

Thank you for your help cataloging all the Bukakkemon.

Share your finished coloring pages with me on social media!

Use #Bukakkemon and tag me.

On Twitter:
@AlexisHex

On Instagram:
@alexis.hex

Also find me on YouTube:
youtube.com/user/alexishex

Until next time, Stay Hexy!